THE MANUAL OF
INTERIOR PLANTSCAPING

THE MANUAL OF INTERIOR PLANTSCAPING

A GUIDE TO DESIGN, INSTALLATION, AND MAINTENANCE

Kathy Fediw

LEED AP ID+C, CLP, CLT

TIMBER PRESS

PORTLAND, OREGON

The Haseltine Building
133 S.W. Second Avenue, Suite 450
Portland, Oregon 97204-3527
timberpress.com

Printed in China

Cover design by Anna Eshelman
Text design by John Hubbard

A catalog record for this book is also available from
the British Library.

Library of Congress Cataloging-in-Publication Data

Fediw, Kathy, author.
   The manual of interior plantscaping: a guide to design,
installation, and maintenance/Kathy Fediw.—First edition.
       pages cm
   Includes bibliographical references and index.
   ISBN 978-1-60469-557-1
   1. Interior landscaping. 2. House plants. I. Title.
   SB419.25.F43 2015
   635.9'65—dc23   2015019429

This book is dedicated to the two men in my life:

To my dear husband, Ted, the light and love of my life.
You said we would go places, and we certainly have.

And in memory of my dad, Donald B. Johnson,
who passed away shortly after I began writing this book.
You are deeply missed.

Contents

Preface

I confess—I am a big lover of indoor plants. I have personally seen, time and time again, what plants can do for an indoor space and the people who work and live in those spaces.

I remember when my uncle was living in a nursing home back in my home town of Pittsburgh. He was a cantankerous sort with no friends, who sat in his wheelchair in his room every day, moving a few steps forward, then a few steps back, over and over again. During one of my visits I brought him a small plant, with the hopes that it would last longer than a cut flower arrangement. We talked for a while, and then I left to catch a flight back home to Texas.

On my next visit, I walked in his room and he immediately said, "Look at my plant!" Someone had moved his plant to a windowsill and was taking care of it for him. It was his pride and joy, and although he could barely see with cataracts, it brought a sense of hope and happiness into his life. I believe that little plant acted as a bridge between him and his caregivers that would not otherwise have existed.

One plant, one person. Imagine that experience multiplied thousands and thousands of times over, every day.

I believe that if architects and designers know how to creatively add plants to indoor spaces, they will do so during the design phase, not as an after-thought once the furniture is in place. And I believe that if interior plantscapers are inspired and shown how to develop more creative, innovative designs, they will wow their clients and be able to work more closely with the design community.

Interior plantscaping has undergone a lot of changes since I first began working in this field in 1979. But some things never change. Plants are still beautiful, and they still touch us emotionally in ways that nothing else can. It is my hope that this book will be a bridge between the design community and the horticulture community, so we can all work together to make plants a part of our every day lives.

One plant, one person. Repeated over and over again. That's all it takes.

Introduction

Interior plantscaping can be a complicated field, and this book has been written to make things simpler and easier for designers, architects, building owners and managers, landscape architects, and horticulturists. Design is integral with horticultural care—neither can be successful on its own.

This book will show you how to design different types of interior plantscapes—atriums, indoor gardens, green walls, potted office plants, color bowls, dish gardens, and terrariums. Basic design principles and the mechanics behind a successful interiorscape are also included. This book will also guide you on how to maintain and care for indoor plants to maintain the design integrity, including watering practices, pruning, plant nutrition, and preventing pests and diseases. By carefully designing and choosing plants described in the plant palette section of this book, you can create an interior plantscape design that is both functional and beautiful for years to come.

What is interior plantscaping? It's the specialized field of designing, growing, and maintaining plants in the indoor built environment. But it's not just throwing together a bunch of houseplants. Interior plantscaping involves carefully thought-out design, matching the perfect plants for the perfect look in very not-so-perfect conditions of artificial light, fluctuating temperatures, and "helpful" people throwing their coffee and donuts into their plants—and that's on a good day. Plantscaping involves keeping these plants looking perfect all the time, not just after a plant care visit but every single day.

Interior plantscaping is a combination of the disciplines of horticulture, interior design, and landscape architecture. It's using plants to set a mood, direct foot traffic, and enhance architectural features. It's providing a natural way to uplift spirits, improve productivity, and brand a company. It's all this and more.

Other terms are often used for interior plantscaping. The term "interior landscaping" is often used in Great Britain and Europe, as well as for larger atrium and indoor garden projects. The term "plantscaping" or "interiorscaping" is sometimes used in the United States and other countries as an abbreviated version. The term "plant hire" is used in countries such as Australia and New Zealand. "Hire" refers to the rental or lease of plants, which are usually not purchased outright by business clients in some countries. Whatever it's called in your part of the world, interior plantscaping is more or less the same no matter where you go.

Most interior plantscape companies will design the project, sell the plants and containers, and then take care of the plants on a regular schedule. Most interior plantscape companies guarantee that the plants will continue to look great, replacing them whenever their quality declines.

Interior plantscaping falls under the umbrella of urban horticulture, and most companies that offer interior plantscaping services also offer other urban horticultural services. This includes patioscaping, rooftop gardens and green roofs, green walls (indoors and outdoors), holiday and special events decorating, and short-term plant rentals. Some companies also offer cut floral arrangements, treescaping and arboriculture services, lawn care, and snow removal. In other words, if enough customers ask for it—they'll do it!

Plants provide much more than a decorative touch to the indoor and outdoor environment. Numerous research projects have proven that plants remove dangerous toxins such as formaldehyde and benzene from the air and convert them into harmless compounds that plants use to manufacture food, something no other organism or man-made product can do. Plants also help lower stress, reduce cold symptoms and headaches, and increase employee productivity.

With the right design, plants provide a living bridge between people and bring them closer together. According to Edward Wilson's theory of biophilia, people are innately drawn to other life forms. Plants bring people together, help them relax, act as conversation starters, and create an environment for cooperation and collaboration.

Indoor plants and interior plantscapes can be found in offices, building lobbies, atriums, hospitals, schools, hotels, shopping malls, high-end retail shops, and the finest homes. They are truly the gift that keeps on giving. Everyone can enjoy indoor plants, whether at home, in the office, at the mall, or on vacation half-way around the globe.

Whether you work in the interior plantscape business, are an architect or designer, or own or manage a building, this book will guide you and inspire you to create beautiful indoor plantings that will continue to delight visitors for many years to come. Enjoy!

1 What Plants Contribute to a Design

Indoor plants play an important role in interior design. They bring in a living element that is portable, growing, and ever-changing, for a fraction of the cost of a new wall or architectural element. They provide function and form while looking beautiful. They can change the ambiance and feel of a space. They add color to complement any décor. They enhance the design without interfering with other important design elements.

PLANTS AS FOCAL POINTS

An indoor plant can act as a focal point, drawing people through the space and towards a specific destination. This can be done in several ways.

Large specimen plants can be used alone to draw attention due to their size. Specimen plants are usually 12 to 14 feet tall or more. Palms, ficus trees, and certain dracaenas are most often grown for this purpose. Large indoor plants may be difficult to find and are usually contracted months in advance with commercial growers. Specimens are usually used alone or with shorter groundcover plants under their canopies.

Plants with unusual forms act as living sculptures and are often used as a focal point. For example, marginata (*Dracaena cincta*) can be grown with interesting twists and bends in its trunks, and eugenias or ficus trees can be pruned into topiary shapes. Keep any other plants in the area simple and low to the ground so the focal plant stands out.

This bent cane plant is the focal point in an indoor garden. The surrounding plants are lower so the bent canes can easily be seen.

Beautiful, large ficus trees make this modern lobby more warm and inviting.

Brilliantly colored cyclamen, mums, and bromeliads welcome visitors to this lobby.

Plants with bright colors can be used as focal points, either alone or in masses. A bed of brightly colored poinsettias draws attention during the holiday season. Vibrantly colored crotons with their yellow, red, and orange foliage are natural focal points, while neon-green pothos and lime-green *Dracaena deremensis* 'Warneckii' catch the eye from a distance and stand out against solid-green foliage plants.

Plants can help to direct the flow of foot traffic in a space and can be used to establish a walkway. Plants also affect how fast people will move along that walkway.

When several different kinds of plants in a variety of shapes and sizes line a walkway, people tend to walk more slowly. There's plenty for them to see and they are drawn to look at each plant along the way. If the walkway is curved instead of straight, they'll slow down even more.

If identical plants are used in a straight row, people are apt to walk quickly. There's not much to see or capture their attention after the first plant or two. This can be helpful in areas where the designer wants people to move through quickly, such as the waiting line in a movie theater or in a busy lobby.

A row of identical aglaonemas lines a busy hallway, encouraging people to move quickly so the area doesn't become congested.

Snake plants mark the entryway to each cubicle, while adding color and interest to a gray interior.

PLANTS CAN FRAME OR SCREEN A VIEW

A plant can act as a picture frame, drawing attention to an object or destination. The usual way to frame such a focal point is by using a symmetrical arrangement of plants on both sides. For example, two identical palms, one on either side, of the directory in an office building lobby will frame the directory and attract the attention of visitors. Similarly, plants can be used to frame a plaque, a doorway, an elevator, a staircase, an entrance, or even a significant piece of artwork, drawing attention and directing foot traffic to the area. A pair of plants can frame a spectacular view from a window or doorway, drawing people's attention outside the indoor space and visually into the outdoor space.

Plants can also block a view that is less than desirable. In an atrium garden, they can hide the mechanics of a fountain, while in a restaurant, they can conceal the water station, or screen off a private dining room from the main dining floor. Plants can be used as drapes to shroud an ugly outdoor view without substantially decreasing the amount of daylight, maintaining the ambiance and feeling of spaciousness while obscuring the view of that ugly parking garage roof.

PLANTS CHANGE THE ACOUSTICS AND MUFFLE SOUND

Plants help to reduce the amount of noise without altering the overall design of the space in several ways. The next time you're in a noisy restaurant, look around the space. You'll see a lot of hard surfaces—walls, floors, windows, furniture—without much cloth or padding to muffle the sound. Any noises reverberate and bounce back and forth, reaching into the corners. People talk louder in order to be heard, and the sound levels rise even more.

Research has shown that indoor plants are effective in absorbing sound at higher frequencies (which are more annoying than lower-frequency sounds), especially in rooms with a lot of hard surfaces and very little upholstery or cloth. Ficus trees, dracaenas, peace lily, arboricolas, and especially heart-leaf philodendron were particularly effective. In addition, the bark mulch on the soil surface was also found to absorb sound (Costa and James 1995b). This research showed that plants improved acoustics by reflecting and diffracting sound waves. Plants with many small leaves, such as ficus trees, tend to scatter sounds as opposed to absorbing sounds, making the interior space less noisy and more inviting.

PLANTS CREATE VISUAL DEPTH AND DELINEATE SPACES

Large, cavernous spaces, such as building lobbies and shopping malls, can seem intimidating and uninviting. People can feel exposed in big, empty spaces, especially in unfamiliar surroundings. Introducing plants can interrupt that space, creating visual depth and breaking the space into smaller, cozier, more appealing areas.

Plants can act as room dividers, creating smaller, more intimate spaces within a building lobby where people can meet and review their notes prior to attending a business meeting. Plants can also be used as portable walls, creating collaboration spaces in an open-concept office without walls. Most plants in individual pots can be moved as the needs of the tenants and visitors change, something most walls cannot do.

Tall bamboo plants and snake plants partition off this large seating area, creating a more comfortable place to relax.

PLANTS VISUALLY LOWER CEILINGS

Tall ceilings can also be daunting and make a visitor feel small and vulnerable. Introducing tall plants with a canopy of foliage into such a setting creates a "false ceiling" by visually lowering the space overhead. Tall, well-spaced ficus trees can turn a large lobby or shopping mall into an inviting indoor garden space. For example, introducing a 15-foot-tall ficus tree in a space with 50-foot ceilings can visually bring the ceiling down to a more manageable 12- to 15-foot height. The heavier the canopy of foliage, the greater the reduction in perceived overhead space.

PLANTS ADD COLOR AND INTEREST

Plants can add splashes and dashes of color to an otherwise monotone setting. We think of plants as being green, yet there are many shades of green. Leaves can vary from deep green to olive green, blue-green, silver-green, or neon-lime green, to name a few possibilities.

Just as spices add interest to a meal, plants add color and interest in subtle or more vivid ways. Leaves can be variegated white, silver, yellow, red, purple, or orange, or even have markings in multiple colors in the case of croton foliage.

 Tall palm trees and shorter tree ferns effectively bring the visual ceiling of this space down to a more comfortable level in two stages. The airiness of the canopy keeps these two levels from being too heavy.

Vibrant-colored plants stand out while darker shades of green or deep maroon recede, adding depth and acting as a background in plant groupings. Juxtaposing plants of different shades adds more allure and visual appeal in masses of plants.

The vivid colors of the bromeliads and dracaenas stand out along the edges of the planting, while the darker foliage of spathiphyllums in the back recedes, creating depth. Note the contrast and interest created by the white flowers of the spathiphyllums.

PLANTS IMPROVE ECONOMICS AND PERCEIVED VALUE

Research has shown that when plants are present in a shopping area, people perceive that the value of the merchandise being sold is greater, compared to the same merchandise in an area without plants. In one study, consumers were willing to spend a conservative 12 percent more for products in an environment with trees (Wolf 2002). People also tend to linger longer and buy more merchandise in shopping areas where plants are present. Many shopping malls and boutique shops take advantage of this effect to increase sales.

Plants add a sense of luxury and prestige to a space. People subconsciously associate tropical plants with success, and feel more confident working and dealing with companies that have plants in their built environment.

Ferns, palms, and flowering plants are especially effective in creating a luxurious ambiance. These plants are often used in the finest hotels, restaurants, and high-end luxury homes. Most successful corporate headquarters and prestigious office buildings have indoor plants.

A graceful raphis palm adds a touch of elegance to a very traditional home.

PLANTS ENHANCE THE DESIGN AND CREATE AMBIANCE

Indoor plants and their containers act as accessories in the interior design. They add to the overall design and help to create the overall look and feel of the space. For example, cactus and succulents add a southwestern feel to hotels in Phoenix or

A planter of cast-iron plants (*Aspidistra*) adds just the right amount of modernism to a contemporary lobby.

San Antonio. Palms add a sense of luxury and exclusivity to shops in Beverly Hills. Tall, sculptural marginatas and mass canes add the right touch to a contemporary, minimalist office design in New York. Ficus trees and arboricola bushes mimic the outdoors and create a sense of casualness and family-friendly atmosphere in a shopping mall in Cincinnati.

PLANTS CLEAN THE AIR AND CONTRIBUTE TO A HEALTHY ENVIRONMENT

Plants provide a wealth of health and well-being benefits to those who work, live, and visit the indoor built environment. Over the years, scientists and researchers have proven what we've known all along—plants make us feel better.

Plants remove harmful volatile organic compounds (VOCs) such as formaldehyde and benzene from the air, converting VOCs into harmless compounds that plants then use for food. Bill Wolverton, former research scientist at the U.S. National Aeronautics and Space Administration (NASA), was among the first to study this process. Since then, other scientists in several different countries have continued and expanded this research, all with similar results.

Researchers have found that the potted-plant microcosm (the plant, its root system, soil microbes, and soil medium) is able to reduce by at least 70 percent all high-concentration, air-borne VOCs within 24 hours, sometimes completely eliminating these VOCs (Wood et al. 2006). A microcosm's ability to rid the air of VOCs becomes more efficient each time that additional VOCs are introduced in the air, and is equally effective during the day or at night. The VOCs are converted into carbon dioxide and water, along with other harmless compounds. So far, all of the plants researched have shown the ability to reduce all of the VOCs tested to date.

Plants have also been shown to reduce levels of carbon monoxide from indoor air by 90 percent (Tarran et al. 2007). Even at minute concentrations, carbon monoxide can affect attention, focus, and overall health, and can be fatal when in larger concentrations.

Besides eliminating harmful VOCs from the air, plants benefit our health and well-being in many other ways. When plants are in an office space, the occupants experience 40 percent fewer coughs, 30 percent fewer sore throats and dryness in the throat, 30 percent fewer headaches, a 25-percent reduction in dry skin irritations, and a 20-percent reduction in fatigue (Fjeld et al. 1998). In similar research studies, sick leave absences were reduced by an incredible 60 percent in offices with plants (Fjeld 2002). Other research studies have shown that when people are working in a windowless room with plants, they have lower blood pressure and feel more attentive than those working in the same room without plants (Lohr et al. 1996).

Potted plants stabilize humidity and temperature, creating a more comfortable and healthy environment (Costa and James 1999). In fact, plants stabilize the humidity levels indoors to between 30 and 60 percent, the comfort level for people (Lohr and Pearson-Mims 2000). Without plants the humidity levels in many buildings would be an arid 20 percent. Lohr and

Pearson-Mims also proved that potted plants reduce dust levels.

PLANTS INCREASE WELL-BEING AND PRODUCTIVITY

Plants affect our overall sense of well-being in other ways, too. They help to provide feelings of pleasure, calm, and relief from "attention fatigue" and create a restorative environment (Shibata and Suzuki 2002). Designers take advantage of this benefit by using plants in break rooms and restaurants in office buildings and hospitals.

Visual contact with nature reduces the fatigue associated with intense concentration. Plants can help to replenish the attentional system so people can refocus quickly after short "nature" breaks (R. Kaplan and S. Kaplan 1990, S. Kaplan 1995). In another study, college students under stress from an exam felt more positive and had less fear and anger when they had a view of plants (Ulrich 1979).

Plants can also improve our productivity, an important benefit in the workplace. One study showed that people working in a room with plants completed a series of computerized tasks 12 percent faster than those working in the same room without plants (Lohr et al. 1996).

So plants fulfill many needs in the interior design and function of a building. They cost less than expensive artwork, and far less than the construction costs of building new walls or lowering the ceiling. Yet they contribute so much more, improving our health, lowering our stress, and improving the way our brain works. No other living element in the built environment gives back so much while looking beautiful.

Design Basics

Designing with plants is much like painting or any other form of art. Plants are your pigments, and the indoor space is your canvas. Learning the fundamentals of art and design will help plans become more creative, innovative and professional. Knowing where to place plants will help the entire space to function better for visitors and tenants alike.

HOW INDOOR PLANTS ARE SOLD AND SPECIFIED

To develop a workable, practical design, it's important to first know how plants are grown and sold. Planters and decorative containers need to have certain dimensions for the root ball of a plant to fit, both in width and height. Other mechanics must also be considered to allow for water drainage and other plant needs.

Indoor plants are grown in standard-sized plastic pots known as "grow pots." Plants are sold by the pot size, not necessarily by height. The pot size is the inside diameter at the top of the pot, measured in inches in most countries (a few countries use the metric system instead). Most grow pots taper slightly inward towards the bottom and have drainage holes at the sides near the bottom of the pot. Some smaller-sized pots may have drainage holes on the underside or bottom of the pot.

In the United States, the pot sizes most often used in the interior plantscape are 6 inch, 7 inch, 10 inch, 12 inch, 14 inch, and 17 inch.

Sometimes 8-inch pots are also used. Plants in 4-inch or smaller pots are usually not used in interior plantscapes, with the exception of orchids and a few other specialty plants.

Plants in pots that are 21-inches in diameter or larger are referred to as specimen plants. Often metal outdoor landscaping pots, wooden crates, or burlap wrapping are used on the root balls of specimen plants. Specimen plants are usually more than 12 feet in height.

Plants used for interior plantscapes are top-quality and shade-acclimated to do well indoors. Their quality is usually much better than what discount retail stores usually carry, although they may look similar at first glance. Top-quality plants have strong-colored leaves that are at a 45-degree angle to the floor or nearly parallel to the floor. They have strong, well-established root

Aglaonema 'Silver Bay' in the center of this planter has acclimated quite well. Notice how most of the foliage is almost parallel to the floor and overhead lighting. New leaves stand vertical and will eventually fall into a horizontal position as they acclimate.

systems. If you tug on their stems, they remain firmly planted in the pot. The soil should be slightly moist to the touch but not spongy. There should be no gnats or other insects visible.

Plants grown for the interiorscape are moved under shade cloth in increments of increasing density, especially during their last few months and weeks at the nursery, so they will adapt more easily to the indoor environment. This gradual shift to lower light levels helps them adjust better once indoors.

UK pot sizes

In the United Kingdom, pot sizes are expressed by the inside diameter at the top of the pot (in centimeters) or by volume (in liters).

Common sizes are as follows:

Size in liters	Diameter in centimeters
1 liter	13 cm
1.5 liters	15 cm
2 liters	17 cm
3 liters	19 cm
5 liters	22 cm
7.5 liters	26 cm
10 liters	28 cm
15 liters	32 cm
20 liters	37 cm
25–30 liters	40 cm
50 liters	50 cm (for specimen plants)

Plants will lose some height when they are planted in gardens. Garden designs may include bowls and containers of plants sitting on top of the soil to add height and interest, especially if the planter is not deep enough to accommodate the taller root balls of larger plants.

Unfortunately, there is no quality grading system for foliage plants, so it's imperative to buy plants from a trustworthy source. Interior plantscape businesses often use plant brokers, who regularly visit nurseries and greenhouses to select the best plants for their clients. Or they may work directly with growers whom they have visited and with whom they have a solid working relationship. Specimen plants should especially be hand-selected at the nursery several months or even a year or two before they are needed for a particular project.

Plants that are offered for sale should be of a certain height, depending on the variety and size of the grow pot. Plant heights often vary with the seasons, however, and sometimes plants are sold while they are still growing and are below height standards, because they are needed right away. Most nurseries will list the heights as well as the grow pot size for their plants.

Plant height is measured in inches or feet from the ground up, including the height of the grow pot itself. If a plant will be removed from its grow pot and planted directly into a garden, order a taller plant to accommodate sinking the grow pot. When specifying plants in a design, be sure to include both the pot size and the height, especially for larger floor plants.

Plants that are grown in cane form, such as mass cane (*Dracaena fragrans* 'Massangeana', also known as corn plant), are specified by the pot size and overall heights of the canes, measured at the top of the wooden cane trunks themselves. These are sold in standard sizes, too, with the canes usually staggered in one-foot intervals. Allow for an additional 16 to 24 inches in height for the foliage "heads" growing out of the side of the canes near the top. For example, a mass cane that is 6 to 7 feet tall would be sold in either a 12- or 14-inch diameter grow pot, with 4 canes having foliage. It would be labeled as a "5-4-3-2, 12-inch mass cane." The first four numbers indicate the height of each cane, and the last indicates the diameter of the grow pot. In this example, one cane is 5 feet tall from the floor up, another is 4 feet, another 3 feet, and the last is 2 feet tall from the floor up. The overall height of this plant would be 6 to 7 feet tall from the floor up, including the foliage. The photo of *Dracaena fragrans* 'Massangeana' on page 212 shows a 4-3-2, 10-inch mass cane.

The overall height of all plants is measured from the floor up to the top of the majority of the foliage canopy. It does not include any small twigs or single leaves that may stand above the overall silhouette of the foliage canopy.

Kentia palm appears to have a lighter mass than some palms because it has relatively few fronds for its size.

CREATING MASS

In addition to a plant's height and width, its visual weight, or density needs to be considered when deciding where to place that plant in the interiorscape. The number and size of the leaves in the canopy of foliage are what creates mass and gives body to a plant. Some plants have a denser canopy than others. The visual effect of mass is created by the overall density of the foliage canopy.

For example, Kentia palm (*Howea forsteriana*) has just a few fronds. It has a light, airy mass and feel. Chinese fan palm (*Livistona chinensis*) also has just a few fronds, but its fronds are very large, so it has a denser canopy and a visually heavier mass. Areca palm (*Dypsis lutescens*) usually has a larger number of smaller fronds, similar to Kentia palm, but because it has more fronds it also has a denser mass.

Similarly, weeping fig (*Ficus benjamina*) has a dense canopy of small leaves and a heavier mass. As it adjusts to lower light levels, it may lose much of its foliage, resulting in a lacier look and a lighter mass.

TEXTURE

Another element of good design is texture. The visual texture of a plant is a result of the size of its individual leaves. The larger the leaf, the coarser the texture. Fan palms have a much coarser look than Kentia palm, which in turn has a coarser look than areca palm. Fiddleleaf fig tree and rubber plant, with their large leaves, have a much different look and ambiance than their finely textured cousins, weeping fig trees.

Generally speaking, coarse-textured plants are used most often in casual settings and in large spaces, such as atriums. They are often used as a backdrop to more finely textured plants in gardens. Large plants with large leaves tend to stand out more, and are often used as focal points in garden designs.

Finely textured plants, on the other hand, are often used in more formal, classic, elegant designs. They are often associated with Victorian times and are thought of as being more "feminine." Finely textured plants are usually used toward the front edges of gardens where they are more visible.

To keep the design more interesting, vary the texture of plants in groups or garden settings. This adds more interest and can create a sense of depth. Keep in mind that the containers will add texture, too.

SYMMETRY AND BALANCE

Plants can be used to create a sense of balance and symmetry within an interior space in several ways. First, the plants themselves should be in balance with each other. Second, plants can also be used to balance out another fixture in the space. For example, a large sofa in the far corner of a room can be balanced by an equally large plant (or its equivalent mass of several smaller plants) in the opposite corner, thus visually balancing the entire room.

Symmetrical placement of identical plants creates a sense of formality and tradition and works best in conservative settings. Asymmetrical placement is far more interesting but can be harder to accomplish without looking amateurish. Maintaining balance is very important with asymmetrical designs. For example, a large plant on one side of an entryway can be balanced with a grouping of two or three smaller plants on the other side. The total mass of the canopies of the plants on each side should be equal in order to create a sense of balance. Otherwise, visitors will feel as though they're going to topple over every time they approach the doorway. In this example, the single plant should be larger and appear heavier than any one individual plant on the other side.

SCALE, PROPORTION, AND FUNCTIONALITY

Just as plants must be visually balanced within a room, they also need to be in proportion to the room and its other fixtures. Plants should never take away from the functionality of the space where they are located, yet they need to be large enough to be noticed and not get lost. A single small plant will be out of place in a large atrium. Likewise, a very large plant can overwhelm a small space. Generally speaking, larger spaces can accommodate larger masses of foliage. In offices, plants should be at least a foot shorter than the ceiling so they don't overwhelm the space.

People must be able to comfortably walk around a plant without dodging the branches or leaves. So the width and the height of the lowest branches must also be considered. For safety reasons, the bottom branches should be no lower than 6 to 7 feet from the floor. Pruning off lower branches will not only make a tree safer, it also visually makes the tree look taller.

To maintain the functionality of the space and for safety reasons, plants should be kept out of certain areas. Plants should never block an exit sign, fire alarm, fire extinguisher, electrical box, or any other safety equipment. They should be placed at least 12 to 24 inches away from smoke alarms or sprinkler systems. Plants should be kept out of science laboratories or other areas that must be kept sterile. They should never impede walkways or doorways so people can get in and out safely, especially in an emergency. Plants should also be kept out of the way of light switches, vending machines, refrigerators, or other fixtures used often by visitors. People will bump into plants, tear off branches, or try to move plants on their own if they are in the way, causing damage to the plants that could have been avoided.

KEEPING IT SIMPLE

Many people become overwhelmed when they see how many indoor plants are available and tend to want to use one of each. As with most design work, keeping it simple is the way to go. Too much variety in plant selection is too confusing for the human brain to process. It creates a sense of chaos and winds up looking cheap, instead of adding value to the space.

Working with a limited palette of plant varieties within a particular space usually gives the best results. The smaller the space, the smaller the selection should be. Feel free to use multiples of the same plant variety—just limit the number of different varieties used.

For example, a small 100-square-foot office should only have one or two different plant varieties. In a 200-square-foot office, one floor plant 5 to 6 feet tall and a couple of smaller plants is all the space can handle.

The larger the space, the more plants and the more variety of plants can be used. In a larger atrium garden, limit the number of different plants in each section of the garden. Masses of one plant variety give the viewer a transition and pathway for their eye to follow towards one focal plant, creating a more cohesive design.

This simple design uses masses of plants to draw attention to the main focal point, a large adonidia palm in the center of the planter.

Marginata canes with braided trunks, combined with tall metallic planters, complement this modern, minimalist design.

A planter in a mid-century modern home was recently updated with colorful bromeliads.

FITTING THE OVERALL DESIGN

Plants must fit and complement the overall design theme for the space. Certain plants just naturally fit better into certain design themes.

For minimalist and very modern designs, look for plants with clean, vertical lines that aren't too fussy-looking, or trim bushier plants like arbricola and ficus trees into tight, lollipop topiaries. For traditional and mid-century modern designs, plants that mimic outdoor plants in their appearance and look like trees and shrubs usually work best, as do blooming plants like mums, azaleas,

bromeliads, and daisies. For the elegant designs found in high-end luxury buildings, homes, hotels, restaurants, and resorts, consider lush-looking plants, including orchids, bromeliads, and most palms. Tropical designs found in similar settings also tend to utilize the same plant palette.

Table 1. Plants for selected design themes.

Design style	Common name	Botanical name
Minimalist and Modern	Arboricola (tree)	*Schefflera arboricola*
	Chinese fan palm	*Livistona chinensis*
	European fan palm	*Chamaerops humilis*
	Marginata (cane)	*Dracaena cincta*
	Mass cane	*Dracaena fragrans* 'Massangeana'
	Snake plant	*Sansevieria* species
	Washington palm	*Washingtonia robusta*
	Weeping fig (tree)	*Ficus benjamina*
Traditional and Mid-Century Modern	Arboricola (tree or bush)	*Schefflera arboricola*
	Areca palm	*Dypsis lutescens*
	Bamboo palm	*Chamaedorea* 'Florida Hybrid'
	Cast-iron plant	*Aspidistra elatior*
	Janet Craig dracaena	*Dracaena fragrans* 'Janet Craig'
	Peace lily	*Spathiphyllum* hybrids
	Pothos (vine)	*Epipremnum aureum*
	Striped dracaena	*Dracaena deremensis* 'Warneckii'
	Weeping fig (tree or bush)	*Ficus benjamina*
Elegant	Areca palm	*Dypsis lutescens*
	Boston fern	*Nephrolepis exaltata* 'Bostoniensis'
	Kentia palm	*Howea forsteriana*
	Lady palm	*Rhapis excelsa*
	Majesty palm	*Ravenea rivularis*
	Ming aralia	*Polyscias fruticosa*
	Neanthe bella palm	*Chamaedorea elegans*
	Peace lily	*Spathiphyllum* hybrids

Using Floor Plans and Digital Photography

It's fairly easy to design an interior plantscape when the building is completed. The designer can walk around the space and decide where the plants should go, how big they should be, and which varieties would do best in the lighting that is available.

It's a completely different situation, however, when the building is still in the design phase or is under construction. Then the designer must rely on floor plans to help in deciding where to place plants, and which plants to specify for the space. Floor plans are also helpful when designing a very large space, an atrium, or a very complex design.

The interiorscape client, the decision-maker who decides which design and which company to use, needs to be able to visualize what the space will look like with the plants selected. Building managers, office managers, architects, and designers are accustomed to seeing detailed floor plans, idea boards, digital photographic designs, and other supporting documents frequently presented by interior designers and architects. The more complex the design, the more supporting documents will be expected by the decision-maker.

A well thought-out floor plan will help the designer work out any logistical problems before money is spent on plants, containers, delivery, and other costs. Ceiling heights, exits, window placement, utilities, lighting, and other factors all need to be considered when deciding where plants will be placed.

Using a floor plan helps the designer look at plant placement from a different perspective and shows what needs to be changed, creating a design that looks more unified and professional, even if no one else sees it but the designer. Floor plans are also an important tool for the delivery and installation crew, especially if the designer is not able to meet them at the job site. The crew leader should be trained on how to read a floor plan so they and their team can deliver the design that the customer approved efficiently, accurately and safely.

READING A FLOOR PLAN

A floor plan is a diagram of what a space would look like if viewed from the ceiling downward. Symbols are used to identify furniture, lighting, walls, windows, doors, and so on. Usually there are several floor plans for a space, depicting different aspects of the design, each tailored to the needs of different contractors.

For example, one floor plan may indicate the electrical work, fixtures, and outlets. Another may depict the plumbing and its fixtures. Still another may indicate the lighting fixtures and its electrical system. Another may indicate the heating system and its duct work, and so on.

The floor plan used primarily for interior plantscaping is the furniture layout, which shows the placement of furniture and other related items in relationship to the walls, windows, and doorways. If possible, look at the other plans as well to get a better overall idea of the conditions in which the plants will be placed.

Standard symbols are used by designers and architects to depict furnishings and other fixtures in the interior design. Most look like the outline of the object if seen from overhead. Others, however, don't look anything like what they represent.

PLACING PLANTS USING A FLOOR PLAN

Indoor plants do best when they receive natural sunlight, so placing plants in a window is ideal. However, plants may block an otherwise spectacular view, so in that case it may be necessary to place plants off to the side of window. Unfortunately, placing plants to the side, window tints, drapes or blinds, an overhang, or buildings directly outside a window will reduce the amount of light significantly, often by 50 percent or more.

If placing plants in windows is not possible or is impractical, the next best source of light will be from artificial light fixtures. Place plants under light fixtures whenever possible. However, plants should be at least 12 inches away from hot lamps and bulbs so the foliage does not get burned.

Keep plants out of traffic patterns. Be sure to leave plenty of space for people to walk past with a minimum 30 inches of walkway space. The safety of tenants and visitors must be the top priority at all times. Maintaining a walkway space keeps people from getting injured by overhanging leaves or branches, especially if they are at eye level. In case of an emergency, people need to be able to quickly and safely exit the building, unimpeded by plants. Likewise, emergency personnel need to have easy access to all parts of the building. And the space simply won't work if there isn't enough room for people to move about freely.

In addition, keeping plants out of traffic patterns preserves their longevity. Plants are easily

This typical floor plan shows partitions, doorways, furniture, plants, and an in-ground planting area.

damaged by people brushing up against them, bending their leaves and stems. Plants will look better for a longer period of time if they are protected by allowing enough space for people to comfortably walk past.

Plants should also be placed where horticulturists and delivery crews can work safely. I've seen plants on high ledges that required workers to wear safety harnesses when placing and caring for the plants. Most green walls that are more than one story high include the design of a mechanical lift for safe plant care and maintenance. Plants on

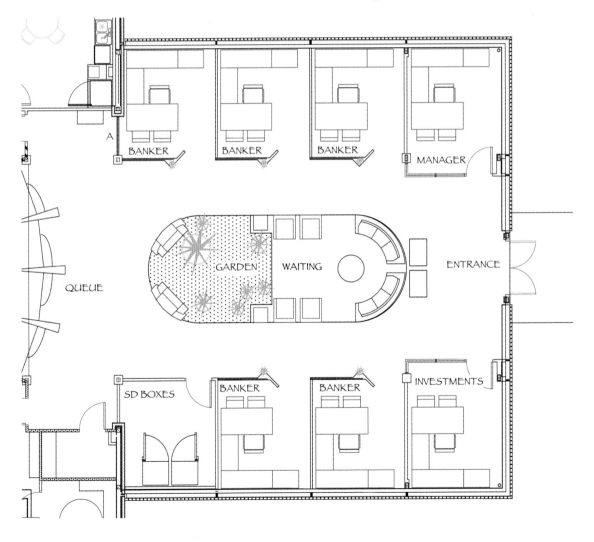

ledges above doorways, especially rotating doors, are also difficult to safely place and maintain. In some cases, consider using designer-quality artificial plants, or designing support structures and safety elements such as platforms and hand-rails to make care and installation safer and easier.

Placing plants near outdoor exits exposes them to extremes in temperature and the weather. Plants should be placed well to the side of exterior doorways or behind a protective barrier to keep them looking great. Choose plants that are more tolerant of extremes in temperature, especially colder temperatures in areas where that's an issue. Many new varieties have been bred to be cold-tolerant, holding up well when exposed for short periods of time to temperatures of 40 to 50 degrees Fahrenheit. Certain new *Aglaonema* varieties, such as 'Silver Bay', are more cold tolerant that older varieties. Other plants that are more cold-tolerant

▼ This is what the design looks like once the plants have been added.

include arboricola tree (*Schefflera arboricola*), sago palm (*Cycas revoluta*), cast-iron plant (*Aspidistra elatior*), and English ivy (*Hedera helix*).

Keep in mind that most indoor plants are subtropical or tropical in origin and don't like to be exposed to temperatures below 50 degrees Fahrenheit for long periods of time. If exposed to temperatures below freezing, plant cells burst and are destroyed, resulting in black or bronze markings and dead leaves on the areas exposed to freezing temperatures. A few minutes are all it takes to permanently damage a plant. Plants such as

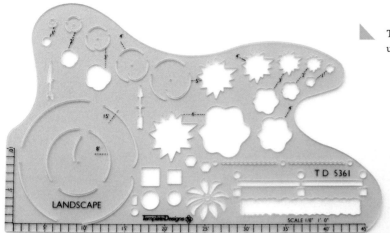

This landscape template by Avery can be used for hand-drawn planting designs.

dracaenas and aglaonemas, if exposed to lower temperatures, will often flower, which frequently ruins their symmetrical growth and may attract insects, especially ants. Many people find their fragrance to be overpowering and too sweet.

Once the space has been evaluated—the pedestrian walkways, placement of windows, ceiling height, doorways, and so on—decide on the locations of plants and mark them on the floor plan. Software program such as AutoCAD, Redit, or Photoshop can be used, depending on the level of expertise and if the plan will be used in a formal presentation.

If the design plan will only be seen by designer and installation crew, hand-drawn placement of plants on the floor plan may be all that is needed. Symbols can be drawn free-hand or by using a landscape template, which is easily affordable and can be found on the internet. Use tracing paper or vellum first, laying the paper on top of the floor plan. This is very helpful for trying out different combinations or locations for plants. The designer can compare designs before choosing which one to use.

Many of the symbols used by landscape architects for outdoor landscapes can also be used for interior plants. The shape should approximate the overall outline of the plant variety and should be drawn to the same scale as the floor plan. Most floor plans are drawn to a scale of ¼ inch or ⅛ inch—purchase landscape templates for both scales.

Treelike indoor plants with a single trunk would be represented by one of the symbols commonly used for trees. Shrublike plants, generally 2 to 4 feet tall with multiple stems and no single visible trunk, would be represented by one of the symbols for shrubs. Palms would use the palm symbol found on the template. Ferns can also be represented by the palm symbol. Ground cover plants, such as pothos, would use one of the ground cover templates, as would masses of flowering plants.

For masses of the same plant, draw overlapping shapes. Use a small + symbol to show the center of each plant, and eliminate the interior outlines, keeping only the exterior outline of the mass as one continuous line.

On the floor plan include a line pointing to each plant with its name, pot diameter, and height. On more complicated floor plans, label each plant with a code and include the code at the bottom of the plan or on a separate page.

Include a complete plant inventory with a listing for each space or area, the quantity, size and variety of each plant. Remember to keep it as simple as possible while supplying enough information to guide the installation crew, and inform the client of what exactly they are purchasing.

Designers may use landscape symbols to indicate the placement of plants.

Neoregelia Medusa or similar 6" container
Qty: 10 changed a minimum of 4 times per year

Sanseveria laurentii 10: 30" ht.
Qty: 13

Pheonix roebelinii 23" container
Single Stem 6– 8 ft. ht.
Poly pebble mulch under Pheonix.
Protoast mulch elsewhere
Qty: 2

Botanical Accent™ changed a minimum or 6 times per year
planted in an Ovation Tall Planter (OVAT-271852) surrounded by
9 Anthirium "Polly" 6" container.

Note: there are two entrance atria. The quantities listed are for one atria only.
Not to Scale

Digital photographs help clients envision what they are purchasing.

Digitalphotographsthatincludeshadowsand other details look more realistic and make a more effective sales tool.

RENDERINGS AND DIGITAL PHOTOGRAPHY

Clients also expect to see a digital photograph of what their space will look like with the plants and containers in place. Some artistic designers prefer to do hand sketches, but most clients prefer to see a digital image of what they'll be getting. In fact, some clients will not accept proposals without digital images.

Fortunately, this is fairly easy to do with today's software. Companies such as Tropical Computers have digital photographs of hundreds of plants, containers, and related items at a very reasonable fee. These can be used with Photoshop or similar imaging software to show what the space will look like with plants.

To produce a digital image, move out any plants or other fixtures that are being eliminated and take photographs of the space with a digital camera. Unwanted plants can be removed digitally from a photograph, but it's easier to take the photograph without them in the way. Copy and paste from the library of digital images, placing them in the exact location of the proposed plants. Be sure the plants are to the same scale as the rest of the items in the digital image and appear true-to-size. Add shadows or adjust the color if necessary to make the digital images as realistic as possible.

Many designs today incorporate digital photography with schematic drawings. This gives the client an accurate picture of what the planting will look like, while providing some of the details necessary for the installation team.

A digitally rendered drawing gives a client an accurate picture of what the project will look like.

Choosing the Right Plants: Lighting Requirements

Besides choosing plants based on their design characteristics, the designer must also consider a plant's lighting requirements. Plants are living creatures and they need light to survive and thrive, whether they are indoors or outdoors.

Plants primarily use light for the process of photosynthesis. In very simplistic terms, light energy is used to convert water and carbon dioxide from the air into food in the form of carbohydrates. Plants then use carbohydrates to fuel the growth of new cells as well as other metabolic processes necessary for their survival.

All of this takes place within the chloroplasts, grainy parts of a plant's cell that contain chlorophyll, a green substance that gives plants their color. Most of a plant's chloroplasts are located near the upper surface of a leaf where they can catch the most available light. Although some chloroplasts can also be found on the underside of a leaf, they usually aren't in large enough quantities for plants to survive based on underlighting alone. Directing a light from underneath a plant may look dramatic, but it's not enough additional light to make much of a difference to the survival of a plant.

Over time, a plant will re-orient its leaves and stems towards its major source of light, a process called phototropism. It looks like the plant is bending towards the light, but actually the cells on the "dark" side are growing more rapidly than those on the "light" side, making the plant grow crooked. This occurs because the shaded side of the plant has a higher concentration of auxin, a plant hormone that promotes cell division, elongation, and growth (Greulach and Adams 1975). Plants are innately programmed to survive and make the best use of the resources available, especially light.

Plants use light energy that is primarily in the red and blue wavelengths for their growth and survival. The rate of photosynthesis peaks around 430 nanometers (blue) with a secondary peak at 670 nanometers (red). (A nanometer is a microscopic measure of length equal to one billionth of a meter.) The rate of chlorophyll synthesis is nearly opposite, peaking at 655 nanometers (red) and again at 400 nanometers (Gaines 1977). Interestingly, our ability to see light peaks around 550 nanometers (green), making green the easiest color, and the most restful color, for our eyes to see. Many hospitals paint their surgery and recovery rooms a pale green, and green is used in the waiting room for entertainment venues. This may also explain why we are drawn to green plants.

Photosynthesis stops when the lights go out and plants are in the dark, but if temperatures are too high, over 115 to 120 degrees Fahrenheit, plants will also stop manufacturing food even if the lights are on. The stomates (specialized structures similar to the pores on our skin) on the leaves close up. This stops the exchange of gases and water vapor in and out of the plant so the plant doesn't die from dehydration, another survival mechanism. When the stomates close, photosynthesis also stops.

Leaves may curl inward when a plant is too dry. This is another survival mechanism as the plant tries to minimize the amount of water lost through its stomates, a process called transpiration. If plants are exposed to high temperatures for long periods of time, they will stop growing and

Dehydration is causing the fronds on these palms to droop and curl inward in an effort to minimize the loss of water.

start declining since they can't manufacture enough energy for their survival.

Different plants need different levels of light to do their best. Most plants grown indoors originate on the floor of subtropical jungles and are already genetically suited to living in minimal amounts of light. Plant breeders then develop new varieties that will do even better in indoor lighting conditions. The growers go even further, moving plants into increasing amounts of shade to acclimate them to lower and lower levels of light.

Plants that are highly variegated or vividly colored tend to need more light than those that are solid green. The less green in a plant, the more light it needs. Plants with very little green, such as pink-and-white marginatas, don't do very well indoors—they don't receive enough light to produce chlorophyll for the manufacture of food. In strong light, the variegation becomes more pronounced and stronger, but plants need some green chlorophyll in the leaves.

When a variegated plant is placed in an area where there's not enough light, the variegation tends to fade and the leaves eventually become mostly green. For example, mass cane (*Dracaena fragrans* 'Massangeana') will lose its yellow stripes and become mostly solid green. The variety of the plant and its genetics did not change—it is still a Massangeana. The plant has simply adapted to lower light levels and has become more efficient at capturing and using the limited amount of light available.

Plants will often lose some of their coloring and become paler in response to low light levels. The leaves on this plant are drooping downward because the plant has not been watered for a long time, another reason that plants lose their coloring.

DETERMINING THE AMOUNT OF LIGHT AVAILABLE

A simple way to determine how much light is available and if a particular variety will do well is the "white paper test." Place a sheet of white paper (any type will do) at about the same height as the top of the plant. Place your hand about a foot above the paper, in between the paper and the major source of light.

If the shadow of your hand on the paper is sharp, crisp, and easy to see, strong light is reaching the plant. Plants requiring high light should do well. If the shadow of your hand is visible but the edges of the shadow are soft and difficult to determine, medium-light plants will do well. If the shadow of your hand is fainter with no determinable edges, plants that require low light will live for a long time with proper care. If you can't see the shadow of your hand at all, there is not enough light for a plant to do well. Low-light plants will live for a while but will need to be replaced soon. Medium-light and high-light plants should only be used for temporary or seasonal displays in place for few weeks or less.

The amount of light a plant gets decreases as the plant gets shorter, so a plant that is 6 feet tall may get plenty of light near its top, but a 3-foot plant will get considerably less. Choose plants that require lower light levels when specifying shorter plants.

In addition, the plants receive less light near their bottom, and eventually lower leaves will drop. The top of a 6-foot plant may do well and grow while it continually loses its lower leaves.

MEASURING LIGHT

Horticulturists measure light in terms of foot-candles. A foot-candle (FC) is a unit of light on a flat surface one foot away from the light of one candle. One foot-candle is equal to one lumen per square foot. The lumen is the standard unit of measure for the brightness or intensity of light for light bulbs.

Bright, direct sunlight may be 10,000 FC. Indoor spaces usually range from 10 FC to as much as 500 FC in a bright, sunny window. Most office spaces are 50 to 200 FC, with an average of 125 FC in the interior spaces.

A lux is a metric unit of light and is the equivalent of one lumen per square meter instead of square foot. One foot-candle is approximately equal to 10.76 lux, and a lux is approximately 0.093 FC. In some disciplines, a lux is called a meter-candle.

Horticulturists use a foot-candle light meter to measure the amount of light a plant will be receiving. Many interior plantscapers who have been practicing their craft for a number of years use an older model from General Electric, Model Type 217, which measures light in 3 different foot-candle ranges and has a side switch to go from one range to the other. It also comes with a metal light diffuser that fits like a cap over the light sensor on top of the meter, to drop the amount of light being measured by 10 times. The light diffuser is useful outdoors where light levels are frequently 1000 FC, the highest amount otherwise measurable on this meter. Light meters last a life time if they are not dropped or damaged and used light meters can sometimes be found for sale on the internet. This model is also color and cosine corrected for using with plants.

Light meters are used by designers and horticulturists to measure the amount of light a plant is receiving in foot-candles.

Newer models of foot-candle light meters are digital and range widely in price, from $20 to several hundred dollars. The less-expensive models are primarily for hobby use and are sometimes combined with a moisture meter. They usually don't give accurate readings in foot-candles, rather they show light on a range from low to high. These ranges, however, have very little to do with most published light requirement categories for plants and should not be used to determine which plants to place.

More expensive models range from $60 dollars and up. The sensor may be built-in or attached to a cord to make it easier to read the light intensity higher up the leaf canopy or deep inside the canopy. These models are very accurate and easy to use. Some models measure in both lux and foot-candles.

Some people try to use their camera or a photographic light meter to measure light. However, most of these are not made to measure light in terms of foot-candles. Consult the camera's instruction book for details on how to convert the measurements into foot-candles.

To measure light with a light meter, hold the meter at the top of the plant and point the sensor towards the major source of light. If using an older model, the light sensor is the frosted plastic piece found at the top of the light meter. Start with the switch at the top level, measuring light between 200 and 1000 FC and read the measurement from the top scale. If no reading shows, lower the side switch to the middle position and look for a reading on the middle scale, from 50 to 250 FC. If there is still no reading, move the side switch the lowest level and read from the lowest scale, 0 to 50 FC.

When using a digital light meter, point the sensor to the primary source of light at the height of the plant. The meter will give a reading for the amount of light the plant is receiving. Next, repeat this process and measure light levels at different levels on the plant to get an idea of how the lower foliage will do in the location. In addition, measure the amount of light pointing the sensor away from the major source of light. For best results and plant longevity, choose plants according to the range of light they will be getting.

Repeat this process several times a year for plants in windows. Take light meter readings during different seasons and times of the day, and in different weather conditions. The results may be surprising and can explain why plants are not doing as well as expected.

NATURAL LIGHT

Placing plants in windows where they can get natural sunlight is almost always preferred. The sun provides all the wavelengths of light that plants need, but the quality and quantity of light that a plant gets, even when it's sitting in a window, can vary greatly depending on several factors.

The amount of light a plant receives can be diminished if there are any overhangs or awnings on the building above the window or if there are buildings in front of or directly across from the window. Any tints or glazes on the glass can decrease the amount of light reaching the plant, as can window coverings, such as blinds, shades, and drapes. Other obstacles, both indoors and outdoors, may reduce incoming light. Finally, if plants are more than 5 feet away from the window, or if

they are taller than the window itself, they may not receive the light they need.

Ideally, plants should be at least one foot shorter than the top of the window, and taller than the bottom of the window. They should be no further away from the window than its height. Most sources agree that plants placed more than 15 feet from a window will not get enough natural daylight to survive (Gaines 1977). Place the tallest plants closest to the window so their tops get the most light, but not touching the glass, which may become too hot on sunny days. Most plants should be placed within 5 feet of a window as the amount of light drastically decreases past 5 feet.

The quality or wavelengths of light is influenced by the type of tinting used on the glass. Many buildings, in an attempt to lower their air conditioning bills, now use tinted windows—great for lowering energy costs but not always good news for plants.

Tints are used to increase privacy, cut back on glare, and reduce the heat produced by sunlight streaming directly into windows. The most common tint colors used are gray, bronze, and blue-green. Some appear transparent from indoors, others show their tint and alter the color of outdoor elements when viewed from inside.

The amount of sunlight transmitted through tinted glass varies with the tint and thickness of the glass. Light transmission can be decreased to as low as 10 percent for highly reflective tinted glass. Most tinted double-paned windows transmit only 22 percent of the outdoor light (University of Minnesota 2011). In comparison, a clear double-paned window transmits up to 78 percent of the light, and a clear single-paned window transmits up to 100 percent of light.

Spectrally selective tints have been developed that decrease the solar heat gain while transmitting more light into the indoor space. These are usually light blue or light green in color and tend to absorb the heat from sunlight, so they are generally used on the outer pane of a double-paned window, so the heat can be transmitted back to the outdoor environment. They transmit the visible wavelengths of light while absorbing the wavelengths that create heat.

The amount of light a plant gets in a window is also influenced by the direction the window is facing. Eastern windows get the morning sunlight and western windows get the hot afternoon sunlight. A compass will help determine which direction windows are facing and is particularly helpful on cloudy days.

Windows that get the morning light will usually support medium-light to low-light plants, but may not provide enough light for high-light plants to do their best. Windows that get the direct afternoon sun are great for high-light and medium-light plants, but the strong sun and higher temperatures may be too much for low-light plants. Windows that get strong indirect light most of the day will support most plants. Windows that get weak indirect light will only support low-light plants.

Plants can also get natural sunlight from skylights, clerestories, and solar tubes. Most people assume that the amount of light a plant gets from an overhead skylight will be very high, but this is usually not true. The higher up the skylight from the ground floor, the less light will actually reach the plant itself. In a 20-story building with an open lobby and skylights in the ceiling, the plants on the bottom floor may only get 25 FC of light or less for most of the day. In a one-story building, the amount of light will be much stronger.

In addition to the distance, the sun may only shine in directly down from the skylight for a couple of hours a day, depending on the latitude, the season and the design of the skylight. The rest of the day the interior will be getting indirect sunlight, since the sun will not be directly overhead.

Having a skylight does not necessarily mean that plants requiring high light will do well on the ground floor. Use a light meter to be sure of the amount of light available, and visit the site on cloudy days as well as sunny days. Sources such as the Illuminating Engineering Society's *Lighting Handbook* are available to help calculate the amount of light a plant will get from a skylight, depending on the well depth, dimensions, glazings, and so on.

ARTIFICIAL LIGHT

The floor space in front of a window is only a small portion of the entire built environment, and often we use plants deeper within the space, far away from natural light. Plants in the inner depths of a building rely solely on artificial light, and their survival depends on the quantity (intensity), quality (wavelengths), and duration of their exposure to light. The intensity and quality of light is determined by the type of light bulb that is used and its distance from the plant.

Most buildings are designed for the comfort and productivity of the people who live, visit, and/or work in those buildings, not for the survival of plants. People are more comfortable with balanced lighting that includes the warmer tones, yellows and oranges, as well as red and blue wavelengths of light. Luckily, the types of light bulbs used indoors usually work well for plants, too. There is no need to use special plant lights or grow-lights for indoor plants.

Fortunately today we have lighting that is more balanced and full-spectrum, some of which are marketed as "natural" light bulbs. We no longer need to choose between healthy plants and comfortable people—both can co-exist comfortably in the same space.

There are many choices when it comes to artificial light, and new technologies are being introduced nearly every year. LED (light emitting diode) light bulbs, also known as lamps, are today's first choice. They are more energy efficient than most other types of bulbs. Their price has been going down as the demand and supply increases. These bulbs can be made in any spectrum of light and can be very effective for plant growth. They last longer than compact fluorescent lights (CFLs) and give off a very intense, bright light. LED lights give off more foot-candles of light per wattage (the measurement of energy used) than incandescent or fluorescent bulbs, while giving the same or better results. They literally never burn out. Eventually they will become less efficient, and most lighting experts recommend they be replaced when they give off 30 percent less light than their original output.

CFL light bulbs last longer than incandescent and tube fluorescent lights but are quickly being replaced by LED light bulbs in popularity as the more energy efficient LEDs become lower in price. Many people also object to the small amounts of mercury found in CFLs, which creates problems for the environment when it is time to dispose of these lights. Bulbs fit traditional lamps and

LED light bulbs are gaining in popularity and use as their price continues to drop. They are the most energy efficient bulbs available for general use at the time of this writing.

fixtures that once took only incandescent bulbs. These lights are more energy-efficient and last longer than incandescent bulbs, but LEDs still remain supreme with a longer life span. Plants do fairly well with CFL lighting.

Tube-shaped fluorescent lights were the first choice for most offices in the 1960s to 1990s. Cool white fluorescent lights provide a good spectrum of light for plants. They are not used as much today due to their relatively high use of energy, difficulty in disposal, and the need for unattractive ballast-style fixtures.

Traditional incandescent light bulbs were at one time used in most lamps, especially in residences. As of 2014 most incandescent light bulbs were phased out of production. They did not meet the EISA (Energy Independence and Security Act of 2007) standards which required manufacturers to improve the efficiency of light bulbs by a 25-percent reduction in their energy use. Energy use is measured in wattage and traditional incandescent bulbs are not able to provide the same amount of lumens with 25 percent lower wattage. Incandescent light bulbs are no longer for sale (except for any pre-existing stock), but you may still have a few around your home. Fortunately, LEDs and CFLs can be purchased to fit current light fixtures and give roughly the same amount of lumens, using much less wattage per bulb. The U.S. government provides these measurements to use when replacing old incandescent light bulbs. The lumens can found on the packaging.

Table 2. Light output of traditional incandescent bulbs.

Incandescent light bulbs (in watts)	Approximate light output (in lumens)
100 watts	1600 lumens
75 watts	1100 lumens
60 watts	800 lumens
40 watts	450 lumens

SOURCE: Data from the U.S. Department of Energy.

Old incandescent light bulbs create too much heat for most indoor plants and do not provide enough light in the red and blue wavelengths for healthy growth. It is best to replace incandescent bulbs, which will burn out sooner or later, with CFLs or LEDs, both to save on energy and to provide a better spectrum of light for indoor plants.

Halogen bulbs are typically marketed as "energy efficient" bulbs and can look like incandescent bulbs. A 29-watt halogen bulb will give the same amount of light as a 40-watt incandescent bulb with a 28-percent energy reduction, just fitting the requirements of the new EISA standards. Their energy savings are minor, however, compared to more efficient CLF and LED light bulbs.

HID (high intensity discharge) bulbs are employed mostly for large indoor areas, outdoor applications, automotive headlights, and industrial use. They give off a very bright light and are more energy efficient than traditional incandescent, halogen, and fluorescent bulbs. They also tend to give off UV radiation that can cause injury to people and animals, so most are equipped with filters. This type of bulb includes high pressure sodium and metal halide bulbs. Their useful life span is much shorter than LED light bulbs. HIDs are rarely used in office spaces but may be found in very large atriums, indoor stadiums, or shopping malls.

LIGHT DURATION AND UNINTERRUPTED DARKNESS

Another factor impacting plant growth is light duration—how long the plants are exposed to uninterrupted light each day. Each plant variety has a light compensation point (LCP), the amount of light required for a plant to manufacture enough food to compensate for the amount of food used for its metabolic processes. Plants need to receive more than the light compensation point to grow and survive. Research has been done on only a handful of plants to determine their light compensation point. Based on experience we can estimate how many foot-candles are needed for maintenance and growth, using 12 hours of light per day as the standard (see Table 3).

If plants are receiving less than the LCP in foot-candles of light, it is possible to make up the difference by lengthening the time they are exposed to light each day. But it's better to match the plants chosen for the space to the amount—and duration—of light available, and that's what indoor plantscapers deal with most of the time. Most plants grown indoors get at least 10 to 12 hours of light per day and their lighting requirements and categorization take this into effect.

Plants also need a certain amount of uninterrupted darkness per day. Such periods provide plants with a rest from the busy work of photosynthesis and growth. During darkness, the rate of respiration exceeds the rate of photosynthesis. During respiration, plants break down all those carbohydrates they manufactured during photosynthesis into energy they can use for growth. The byproducts of this process include carbon dioxide and water, which plants can then use for photosynthesis once again.

In addition, many plants need a minimum number of hours of uninterrupted darkness each night to flower. Those that initiate flower buds when the day length is less than the amount specified for their species are considered short-day plants (or long-night plants). Poinsettias and chrysanthemums are good examples of short-day plants. Even a few minutes of light at night are enough to disrupt their flower-initiating mechanisms. Plants that initiate flower buds when the day length is more than the amount specified are called long-day plants. Many plants don't care; these are considered day-neutral plants.

Some buildings, especially hotel lobbies and shopping malls, choose to leave their lights on 24 hours a day, 7 days a week. If plants are exposed to light constantly without a break, their foliage will eventually "burn out" from having to work all the time. Their leaves don't have a chance to use the energy stored. Instead, they are constantly manufacturing and storing more and more carbohydrates for energy. Their leaves will look bleached out and become completely ineffective at photosynthesis.

Table 3. Light requirements of selected plants.

Light needed* (in foot-candles)	Common name	Botanical name
Low light **(30–150 FC)**	Cast-iron plant	*Aspidistra elatior*
	Chinese evergreen	*Aglaonema* (most varieties)
	Janet Craig dracaena	*Dracaena fragrans* 'Janet Craig'
	Kentia palm	*Howea forsteriana*
	Lady palm	*Rhapis excelsa*
	Mass cane	*Dracaena fragrans* 'Massangeana'
	Peace lily	*Spathiphyllum* 'Mauna Loa' (and others)
	Pothos	*Epipremnum aureum*
	Rikki dracaena	*Dracaena deremensis* 'Rikki'
	Sago palm	*Cycas revoluta*
	Snake plant	*Sansevieria* species
	Striped dracaena	*Dracaena deremensis* 'Warneckii'
	ZZ plant	*Zamioculcas zamiifolia*
Medium light **(150–250 FC)**	Arborea	*Dracaena arborea*
	Arboricola	*Schefflera arboricola*
	Bamboo palm	*Chamaedorea* 'Florida Hybrid'
	Bird's nest fern	*Asplenium nidus*
	Marginata	*Dracaena cincta*
	Philodendron	*Philodendron* (most varieties)
	Reflexa	*Dracaena reflexa*
	Rubber plant	*Ficus elastica*
	Spider plant	*Chlorophytum comosum*
	Umbrella plant	*Schefflera actinophylla*

High light (over 250 FC)	Adonidia palm	*Adonidia merrillii*
	Amstel King ficus	*Ficus binnendijkii* 'Amstel King'
	Bamboo	*Phyllostachys aureosulcata*
	Bird of paradise	*Strelitzia nicolai*
	Black olive tree	*Bucida buceras*
	Ming aralia	*Polyscias fruticosa*
	Peruvian cactus	*Cereus peruvianus*
	Ponytail palm	*Beaucarnea recurvata*
	Pygmy date palm	*Phoenix roebelenii*
	Washington palm	*Washingtonia robusta*
	Weeping fig	*Ficus benjamina*
	Yucca plant	*Yucca gigantea*

*Plants are categorized according to the minimum amount of light they require to survive indoors as measured in foot-candles, based on a 12-hour day. These categories are based primarily on the experience of a number of experts. For this reason not all sources agree and some crossover in categories may take place.

Nurseries grow plants in shade houses to help plants acclimate to lower light levels prior to being sold and used in indoor settings.

Dealing with Plant Growth and Change

In the interior design, most fixtures remain the same from one day to the next until they are replaced with something new. In the interior plantscape, plants are changing daily—growing taller, leaning towards the light, adding new leaves, and dropping old ones. Flowers bloom and die, bearing fruit and seeds if allowed to develop. Soil becomes compacted or decays, sometimes seeming to disappear altogether. Leaves may develop spots or brown edges if bugs, diseases, or nutritional problems come up and they may change color, shape, and size as a plant grows and adapts to its environment.

The interior plantscape is a constantly changing indoor garden of one or many plants. Unlike a sofa or piece of artwork, plants need tender loving care. This is what makes the interiorscape fascinating. This is why people are drawn to plants and feel a connection to them.

The Savannah Theory proposes that people prefer to be in savannah-like environments, perhaps due to the evolutionary development of humans in the savannahs of Africa. This theory can be adapted in the interiorscape to create an atmosphere in which visitors feel most comfortable. In nature, this type of environment includes scattered clusters of trees for shelter from the sun and protection from predators; long-distance views for surveillance of predators; even ground cover to make moving across the terrain easier and more efficient; and a rich diversity of plant and animal species.

Applying these concepts to the interiorscape results in a design marked by groupings of plants; some shorter plants and plants placed within sight for unobstructed views; groupings of lower plants using the same ground cover (top dressing) and containers throughout the space; and a variety of plant shapes, textures, and colors.

ACCLIMATING TO LIGHT

A plant's leaves will change as it adapts to its new environment. Most of that adaptation is the plant's response to much lower light levels than what it enjoyed at the grower's nursery or greenhouse where it was exposed to natural light. This process is called acclimation and usually takes place over the first few months that a plant is in its new home. A plant that undergoes much of its acclimation prior to being delivered to the interiorscape will lose less foliage once it is on the site. Its chances of survival are much greater if it was shade-grown or shade-acclimated.

Shade cloth (screening fabric) comes in several different levels of shading (20 percent shade up to 80 percent shade). In a greenhouse the shade cloth is drawn over rods hanging below the ceiling as a drapery ceiling. Nurseries use shade houses, especially for taller plants. These are open-air, outdoor structures with wood or metal posts and shade cloth hung over the top and sides. Sun and rain still get to the plants, but in varying degrees depending on the shade cloth used. Plants are still fertilized and treated for pests and diseases to grow a premium specimen for interiorscape use.

Plants grown for homeowners are not always shade-grown or shade-acclimated. There is an additional cost involved in growing plants this way, not only in the extra steps taken and in the cost of the cloth, but also in the longer growing time needed to bring a plant to a marketable size. Discount stores usually don't want to pay for this in order to keep their costs and prices lower. Because plants with vertical leaves and thicker canopies of foliage are often not shade grown, these do best when used outdoors for the patio or placed in areas that receive high amounts of direct sunlight.

During the first couple of weeks that a plant is in its new home it "thinks" it's still in the nursery or greenhouse, getting all that lovely sunshine, and therefore its metabolism is still quite high. It takes a few weeks before it realizes that it's in a new place where it doesn't have anywhere near as much light as it was used to getting. This news is quite a shock to a plant. Suddenly its metabolism slows way down, and that's when all the changes start to take place and when problems are most likely to arise.

During acclimation, plants will naturally lose some of their leaves, mostly in the interior and bottom of the foliage canopy. These are leaves that are shaded by the rest of the foliage and not receiving enough light to manufacture the food they need for survival. The process is normal and is usually no cause for alarm. Many plant care companies will remove some of the lower leaves and leaves within the depths of the canopy, thinning out the foliage, prior to delivering new plants in order to avoid some of this leaf-drop. This saves the plant and its new owner from the drama and trauma of leaves falling off, a very good practice to follow. It also helps new plants acclimate more easily by allowing light to reach all the leaves.

Plants will then grow new leaves once it has acclimated to its new home. The new leaves will be different in size, thickness, and shape, resulting in a plant that has adapted to be as efficient as possible in using the light it has available. The leaves will probably be thinner as cells re-arrange themselves in new leaves, making those chloroplasts more exposed to the light. The shape may also change and leaves may become wider to capture more light. In high light conditions, leaves may become larger.

If the new location does not provide enough light for a plant to survive long-term, a different set of changes will occur. New leaves will come out smaller and narrower instead, shrinking down to a size that the plant can maintain with the amount of light available. This is a built-in defense mechanism that allows plants to survive. The leaves may become smaller and smaller as the plant runs out of energy to grow new leaves. Eventually the leaves become so small that the plant no longer looks attractive and must be replaced.

These changes take place during the first six to eight weeks that a plant is in its new home. This is a crucially important time and expert care is needed as a plant adjusts to its new home. Plants are most susceptible to diseases and other problems during their acclimation period.

SLOWING METABOLISM

Plants undergo other changes during their acclimation period, too. All of these responses are part of the acclimation process as the plant adjusts to its new home. Plants don't have the ability to pick up their roots and move to a better location, so because they can't change their environment, they make the most of what they have by changing themselves. Whenever the environment changes, the plant will respond and change again, going through acclimation as often as the environment changes.

In the nursery or greenhouse, plants are heavily fertilized to encourage fast, lush growth. A plant is worthless while it sits in the nursery— it only has value when it reaches a saleable size and is sold. To make money, growers have to grow plants and sell them as quickly as possible. To growers, time really is money.

Plants need and use all that fertilizer when they are in the greenhouse or shade house, but once a plant is indoors, its metabolism slows way down. It doesn't drink as much water as it used to, and it doesn't take up as much fertilizer as it used to. The fertilizer builds up in the soil, sometimes to dangerous levels. Plants may actually start to push water out of their root cells into the soil, instead of taking water in from the soil. The roots become dehydrated and start to die. When roots start to die, the results show up on the leaves and stems and they may start to die, too.

The fertilizer that is taken up into the plant's system gets pushed to the edges (margins) and tips of the leaves, where the cells start to dehydrate as the excess minerals, called soluble salts, begin to build up in the leaf margin tissues. This results in brown tips (called tip burn) and brown edges or margins and is very typical on many kinds of foliage plants. In fact, it is so common that some artificial plant manufacturers color the leaf tips and margins brown to make their plants look more realistic. Flushing out the soil of new plants with fresh water before they are delivered (called leaching) will help to keep this to a minimum.

What is important to remember is that new plants may drink up lots of water the first two or three weeks while they "think" they are still in the

Plants that are not receiving enough light will produce new leaves that are smaller than the old leaves, because the plant does not have enough food or energy to produce larger leaves. This plant will need to be replaced as the newest leaves continue to diminish in size.

nursery or greenhouse, then slow down on their water intake as they acclimate. Knowledgeable horticulturists know to look for this process and change watering practices as their plants acclimate and change.

Some plants naturally take longer to grow and therefore they are more expensive. For example, Kentia palm takes up to 2 years just for the seed to germinate. Then it takes another 2 to 7 years to reach a marketable size, depending on what dimensions the grower is aiming for. Areca palm, in contrast, takes only a few weeks to germinate from seed and then 1 or 2 years to reach a saleable size. No wonder that a Kentia palm often costs at least 3 to 4 times as much as the same-sized areca palm!

LOSE A LEAF—GAIN A LEAF

Plants lose their leaves for a number of different reasons. We have already mentioned how lower leaves may drop if they receive less light and are not able to produce enough carbohydrates for the plant's metabolic processes and survival. Plants may also drop their lower leaves as a response to being too dry. But often otherwise-healthy plants lose their lower leaves because those are the oldest leaves on a plant, and leaves have a life expectancy just like any other living cell or organism. Eventually older leaves die just because they are worn out and old. The average life span for leaves is between 6 months and 2 years.

After a plant acclimates, it eventually reaches a state of homeostasis, or what we might call the Leaf-Light Equilibrium, where it has just the right

amount of foliage to thrive in the amount of light it is receiving. If it grows a new leaf, it loses an older leaf to maintain that equilibrium. The plant cannot produce enough food to maintain the new leaf as well as the older one, so it loses the older, weaker leaf in favor of the healthy, light-efficient new leaf.

One way to encourage new leaf growth is to take advantage of this Leaf-Light Equilibrium and remove older leaves a little at a time to encourage the growth of fresher new leaves. Horticulturists use this technique to keep a plant looking fresh all the time.

Mature Plant Size and Life Span

As long as plants are getting sufficient light, they will continue to grow throughout their life. They will grow new leaves to take the place of old ones as they drop. They will grow taller towards the primary source of light. And in most cases they will also grow wider, too, as stems and branches grow.

Plants will reach a certain height once they attain maturity, depending on their species, but their "mature height" is the height they would be if they were growing outdoors in their natural habitat. Many tropical plants will reach mature heights of 40 to 60 feet or more if they were growing outdoors—a trip to the tropics will show an impressive display of indoor plants being grown outdoors as landscape plants, or in the rainforests where many originate.

In the interior plantscape, plants need to be kept within a size that corresponds to the design of the space. This often means that trimming and

A mature ficus tree growing outdoors will develop a large trunk and many adventitious roots. Its height may reach 30 to 100 feet, depending on the variety and location, and it often is much wider than it is tall.

pruning them is required on a regular basis to maintain the design integrity. Overgrown plants or plants that have grown outside of their desired shape can completely ruin the intentions of the designer, as well as create safety problems. It's always best for the designer to specify plants that will fit the space, not only when they are first installed, but for years to come.

Like all other living creatures, plants have a life span and occasionally an otherwise healthy plant will die simply because it has reached the end of its life span. Most plants die far before this happens, usually because they are no longer attractive and are thrown out. Other plants die before their time from neglect, disease, pests, physical damage, or other causes.

Some plants reach the end of their life cycle once they flower. This is especially true for bromeliads which are often used in seasonal flowering displays. The flower bracts last for several months before they deteriorate and die. This signals the beginning of the end of its life and at this point the plant should be replaced. It may live for a while longer, but it will never flower again and will continue to decline.

Sleek, modern containers complement
the edgy, industrial decor in this hallway.

Individual Potted Plants

The majority of interior plantscape designs center around the arrangement of individual, potted plants. Yet it is the decorative containers that the plants are in rather than the plants themselves that have the greatest impact on the overall design and look of the space.

There are a number of ways to design with individual pots of plants for maximum impact without breaking the budget, and with the array of containers available, potted plants no longer look like they did in the 1960s and 1970s. Back then, plant containers were limited to rattan baskets, terra cotta pots, plastic and ceramic cylinders. Designs were usually very casual and not much more than a hodgepodge mix of mismatched containers, with many different varieties of plants grouped together. Very little effort went into any kind of actual design or planning. The goal was to use as many plants as possible, resulting in a plant "jungle."

As plants became more commonplace in the workplace and corporate offices, designs became more formal and stylized. New containers were manufactured that were waterproof and more aesthetic. Shapes and finishes changed to complement more modern offices. Designers started using fewer plants with one style of container to make their designs more cohesive. Interior plantscapes evolved, and continue to evolve, as new container materials and styles are constantly being developed to meet the needs of the design community.

WHERE TO PLACE POTTED PLANTS

When deciding where to place plants, think about what you want those plants to accomplish within the total design. What role will they play? Will they be a focal point? Aid in directing foot traffic? Act as the backdrop to a seating area? Soften corners? Break up the monotony of an endless sea of cubicles?

Although plants will do best when they get some natural light, they are rarely used in front of windows, particularly in commercial buildings. They may block the view or impede foot traffic if placed directly in front of a window.

Small windowsill plants are usually not used in an office space, primarily because most offices don't have windowsills, and those that do exist are usually not wide enough to safely accommodate a plant. Small plants are also more difficult to maintain and usually require more frequent care, so the maintenance contract for small plants may be beyond the budget of most offices. In addition, small plants on windowsills may look too casual for a business setting and don't give enough visual impact to make them worthwhile.

Corner Plants

Most often potted plants are placed in corners to soften the angles of a room. This esthetically pleasing arrangement makes the space seem more friendly, warm, and inviting. This placement also helps direct people away from the outer walls and corners. The savvy designer knows to place lighting in the corners to brighten the space, and

that helps to keep these corner plants looking their best.

Usually the containers used with corner plants are circular in shape, aiding in the visual "rounding" effect. These containers can be a simple cylinder or shaped like a fishbowl or urn.

Most often corner plant containers are also neutral in color and complement the walls, trim, and/or furniture. Corner plants are not meant to call attention to themselves, but to blend in with the rest of the space and become an integrated part of the design. For this reason, most corner plants are solid green or green with muted color, not brightly colored in either foliage or flowers.

Maintaining the design integrity and keeping plants within the confines of the space are extremely important with corner plants. They must be kept primarily within the circumference of the decorative container, not branching out into the traffic pattern. For this reason most corner plants are columnar and vertical in shape with leaves or fronds that are shorter and attached closely to the main trunks or stems. Cane-form plants, that is, plants with straight, vertical woody stems and tufts or "heads" of foliage at the top, are best used in areas where there is very little space for a plant. Mass canes, for example, have thick wooden stems about 3 inches in diameter with several heads growing from the sides of the cane at the very top. Marginata canes have thinner stems, usually one inch or less in diameter, and may have heads of foliage sprouting at or near the top of each stem. These plants are sold by the height of their canes (their wooden stems) as well as the diameter of their grow pots.

Corner plants also need to be about 6 feet in height or more to be visible above cubicles and other furnishings. Since most corner plants receive

Plants in corners such as this yucca (*Yucca gigantea*) usually have solid green foliage and are in neutral-colored containers, so they will blend in with the overall design of the space.

Cane-form plants such as *Dracaena fragrans* work well in office corners and take up little space.

no sunlight, plants that require very little light such as dracaenas and certain palms are used most often. Favorite selections for corner plants include cane-form plants like mass cane (*Dracaena fragrans* 'Massangeana'), other varieties of *D. fragrans*, and marginata (*D. cincta*), as well as bamboo palm (*Chamaedorea erumpens*) and lady palm (*Rhapis excelsa*).

Desktop and Tabletop Plants

Pothos (*Epipremnum aureum*) works well as a desktop plant. Its vines should be cut back regularly to keep them off the desktop and out of the way.

Size is the primary concern when using a potted plant on a table or desk. People need to have room on their desks to work, plus space for a computer, notes, phone, file folders, and so on. They must also be able to see over and around any plant to talk with visitors and coworkers. To accommodate these needs, smaller plants in 6-inch grow pots are used most often. Their height should be limited to about 12 inches above the rim of the pot.

Vining plants such as pothos are some of the easiest to grow in offices. The vines will need to be kept trimmed back so they don't interfere with work or begin to look messy. They should not be allowed to crawl along the desk or up a cubicle wall. Cutting vines back to within the top of the grow pot will encourage new growth, keeping the plant looking full and compact for a long time. Upright plants will also need to be trimmed back occasionally to keep them from growing too tall.

As always when designing with containerized plants, a waterproof decorative container is crucial. Care must be taken that water does not drip onto important papers or a computer keyboard.

Desktop plants are usually located some distance from a window or other light source, so plants used on desktops are those that do well in low light. Good choices include Chinese evergreen (*Aglaonema*) of any variety, especially compact ones; pothos (*Epipremnum aureum*) vines; philodendron vines; snake plants (*Sansevieria* species), preferably compact varieties; arboricola bushes (*Schefflera arboricola*) in 6-inch grow pots, kept trimmed; ZZ plant (*Zamioculcas zamiifolia*); and compact 'Janet Craig' dracaena (*Dracaena fragrans* 'Janet Craig Compacta').

Tabletop plants are sometimes used instead of flower arrangements in restaurants and break rooms. They last much longer than cut flowers and are more economical in the long run. They also decrease the carbon footprint caused by weekly deliveries of floral arrangements. Because tables in restaurants are used primarily for eating, plant size is more limited. Here plants in 4-inch pots are used more often. Such plants are usually very inexpensive and can be switched out every 3 to 6 months to mark the changes in the seasons, holidays, and special occasions.

Small succulents in a glass jar add greenery and interest to a restaurant table.

 Lower-growing plants such as pothos are often used in rectangular planters to decorate the tops of filing cabinets and shelves. This helps to break up the monotony of open cubicle office plans without taking up any valuable floor space.

In addition to the choices given for desktop plants, good choices for tabletop plants include orchids, kalanchoes, miniature cyclamen, small chrysanthemum plants, azaleas, miniature daffodils and other tiny spring flowers, agaves and other small succulents, and small terrariums.

Plants used on a reception desk need to be somewhat larger and more spectacular than those on desktops. They are often the focal point within a reception area or lobby, drawing people towards the reception desk where they can find assistance. Colorful plants in low containers are used most often and are sometimes combined into "color bowls" with several plants grouped together in the same container (more on this later). Plants in 4- or 6-inch grow pots work well singly or in a color bowl, depending on the amount of space available. Any of the plants listed previously will work well for reception desks.

Filing Cabinet Plants

Potted plants can also be used on top of filing cabinets, shelves, and other storage units. Their size is limited by the width of the unit itself. It is important to leave enough room on top of the unit for people to place file folders and other office items. Allowing for a margin of 12 inches works best.

For units that are at or above eye-level, vining plants and other low plants work best. For units that are below eye level, taller plants may also be used. Rectangular planters with multiple plants work well when space is available. Round bowls with multiple plants, or urn-shaped or cylinder-shaped planters with single plants also work well.

The color of the decorative containers used should match or complement the storage unit for a more cohesive look. The shape and finish of the containers should harmonize with the overall design of the space. Any of the plants recommended for desktops will work well for these locations.

Large ficus trees have visual impact in an atrium, while maintaining a sense of open space.

FLOOR PLANTS FOR LOBBIES AND ATRIUMS

Floor plants (larger plants that sit on the floor either individually or in groups) can make a dramatic impact, especially in a lobby or atrium setting. The plants and their decorative containers must be in proportion to the space. The larger the space, the taller and wider the plants should be. Larger spaces also give the designer more options for creativity in the design.

Individual Floor Plants

Individual floor plants in their own containers can be quite stunning, particularly in smaller lobbies and reception areas. Plants used this way should be at least 6 to 7 feet tall to make an impact and not get lost in the space. People need to be able to move around the plant, so columnar plants such as those used in corners are your best choice.

For larger spaces with taller ceilings (12- to 14-feet minimum ceiling height), tree-shaped plants (with a trunk and canopy of foliage) or palms can be used, provided there is enough space under the canopy for people to walk safely. Plants with an interesting feature, such as colorful leaves or an unusual leaf, trunk, or stem shape, work particularly well. Individual plants are usually used as a focal point or to offset and draw attention to an important design element.

Plants that work particularly well on their own include Kentia palm (*Howea forsteriana*), areca palm (*Dypsis lutescens*), ficus trees, fiddleleaf fig tree (*Ficus lyrata*), arboricola trees (*Schefflera arboricola*), most of the dracaenas grown as canes or tree-form, dracaenas grown with a twist or shape in their canes, and any large specimen plant over 12 to 14 feet tall (for larger spaces).

In larger areas, strategically place individual plants throughout the space. The plants can all be the same, or they can be different, depending on how you intend to use them. The containers should all be the same style, material, and color to draw the overall design together and create a sense of cohesiveness.

A recent trend in floor plants is to use identical, smaller plants in tall, narrow containers in a line

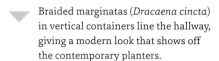
Braided marginatas (*Dracaena cincta*) in vertical containers line the hallway, giving a modern look that shows off the contemporary planters.

near the wall or windows. This creates a very modern look where the star of the show is the container, not the plant. Simple, solid green plants work best with this type of design, such as pothos, ZZ plants, or other short plants. Plants are usually in 10-inch grow pots for this design.

A lady palm (*Rhapis excelsa*) is underplanted with small calatheas and English ivy (*Hedera helix*). Each plant remains in its own grow pot.

Multiple Plants in a Container

Multiple plants can be placed in a single planter, provided the planter is large enough and deep enough to accommodate each plant's grow pot. For floor plants, this usually involves one tall plant, such as a ficus tree or palm, with smaller, 6-inch plants as underplanting. Blooming plants can also be used as underplantings and switched out on a regular schedule to add interest, color, and variety.

Usually each plant remains in its own grow pot. The underplantings may rest on top of the soil of the central plant, provided there is enough room.

Another option is to build a platform that spans the space between the central plant's grow pot and the rim of the decorative container, placing the underplantings on top of the platform. The platform can be built from wood, chicken wire, plastic, or some other material, although this method is rarely used today.

A third option is to direct-plant the central plant into the decorative container. The underplantings, such as pothos vines and similar groundcover plants, can then be direct-planted, too, if they are to remain permanently.

If underplantings remain in their grow pots, they may be double-potted. This alternative involves sinking an empty grow pot or inexpensive cylinder slightly larger than the underplanting's grow pot into the soil medium, then placing the plant in its grow pot inside the empty pot. The plant in its grow pot can easily be lifted out without disturbing the soil medium. This enables the underplantings to be replaced easily with little effort or mess. The rims of the doubled pots are covered with mulch, moss, or other groundcover material to hide the pots. This top dressing or groundcover prevents vandalism and theft and keeps the planter looking natural and professional.

Floor Plant Groupings

Individual floor plants, each in their own decorative container, may also be grouped closely together to create one visual mass of plants. This arrangement creates a good deal of interest that can easily be changed while maintaining the portability of each plant. Individual pots work particularly well with plants that have vastly different watering needs. Groupings of plants also work

A large seasonal planting of spring-flowering plants surrounds a bird of paradise (*Strelitzia nicolai*). Soil medium fills this large planter. The flowers are changed out with the season and remain in their individual grow pots, double-potted and sunk into the soil substrate. The foliage, flowers, and additional preserved moss hide the grow pots.

A grouping of three plants, each with their own underplanting, are in perfect proportion to the space and to each other. The same style of decorative container unifies the design and complements the modern décor, while the rounded organic shape and natural color soften the look of the industrial-styled surroundings.

well for seasonal displays or if the design needs of the space change frequently, such as in a lobby area that is used for special events. The plant groupings provide enough mass to make an impact in a space without the cost of very large or custom-made decorative planters, which often exceed the cost of the plants themselves.

Following some general design principles for plant groupings will greatly enhance the overall effect. First, the decorative planters should all be the same color and finish. They will most likely be different sizes, but keeping them all the same color will act as a unifying agent in the design, much as a lawn of grass acts as unifying agent in the outdoor landscape.

The containers may be shaped differently, but that shape should be limited to two or three at the most. For example, there may be a tall ficus tree in a cylinder-shaped planter, an aglaonema in a cylinder-shaped planter, and pothos in a low dish-shaped planter. The plants are all different sizes and heights, and so are the planters, yet if they are the same color and material the design looks unified.

How many plants should be in a grouping? If space is somewhat limited, a grouping of just two plants may be used. There should be one tall plant and one mid-sized plant 2 to 3 feet shorter. The shorter plant should be placed slightly in front of the taller plant and slightly off-central.

Most of the time a grouping of plants consists of three individual plants. In larger areas, five or seven plants may be grouped together. Always use an odd number of plants for a better design.

The primary rule when grouping plants together is that each plant should be at a different height than the others. No two plants should be the same height unless they are groundcover plants. Ideally, one plant begins where the other ends—in other words, the top of all but the tallest plant should be at or just below the lowest branch or foliage mass of the taller plant. Usually this is indicated by a 2- to 3-foot difference in overall height.

For example, a grouping might consist of a 6-foot-tall *Dracaena fragrans* 'Massangeana' cane, a 3-foot-tall aglaonema, and a bowl with pothos vines. The lowest foliage mass on the mass cane would be around 3 to 3½ feet from the floor, just at the top of the aglaonema. Since aglaonema is an upright plant, its mass of foliage ends at the rim of the pot, about 1½ to 2 feet from the floor. The pothos tops out around 1½ to 2 feet above the floor.

The usual design formula for a grouping of three containers is to use one tall plant in a columnar, cane, or tree form; one medium-sized plant in a ball or fountain shape; and one low container with vining, ground cover, or seasonal blooming plants. In groupings of more than three, additional low containers may be added. If additional medium-sized plants are added, they should retain the same height guidelines and perhaps should be identical plants (three containers of aglaonemas, for example).

In addition, all of the plants in a grouping should provide the same feel or ambiance to the space. A cactus would not look right grouped with palms, and ferns would not look right grouped with yucca canes.

The three pots of plants in this grouping, including the planter behind the peace lily (*Spathiphyllum*), are at different heights. Several small vining plants could be added to the two shortest planters if desired to give more dimension. Notice how the same style of planter and top dressing are used for each planter.

Table 4. Plant combination ideas for groupings of three containers.

Tall container with columnar plant, cane plant, or tree	Medium container with ball-shaped or fountain-shaped plant	Low container with vine, ground-cover, or seasonal-blooming plant
Kentia palm (*Howea forsteriana*)	Chinese evergreen (*Aglaonema* varieties)	Pothos vine (*Epipremnum aureum*)
Mass cane (*Dracaena fragrans* 'Massangeana')	Arboricola bush (*Schefflera arboricola*)	Seasonal flowering plants
Areca palm (*Dypsis lutescens*)	Peace lily (*Spathiphyllum* hybrids)	English ivy (*Hedera helix*)
Lady palm (*Rhapis excelsa*)	Striped dracaena (*Dracaena deremensis* 'Warneckii')	Seasonal flowering plants

PLANTING AND STAGING POTTED PLANTS

Containerized plants take very little water and fertilizer compared to plants in outdoor planters and gardens. They are also less prone to pests and diseases than most outdoor plants, eliminating the need for pesticides. Still, a number of horticultural and design aspects need to be addressed with indoor plants in decorative containers.

Indoor plants need to be watered in such a way that they are not actually sitting in water, which can lead to root rot and a very smelly plant. Yet any drips or spills can cause expensive damage to floors, furniture, and other interior finishes, in addition to creating a safety hazard. Plants need to be changed out easily and with as little mess was possible whenever they start to deteriorate or when a new look is needed. The containers need to

look beautiful and complement the design theme in the space, and any pot rims or other mechanics must be hidden from sight, while keeping the overall look attractive. All of the elements must be easy to install and maintain so both plants and containers look perfect at all times.

Most plants are not direct-planted into the decorative containers by removing them from their grow pots and planting them directly into the planter itself. Instead, most plants are double-potted; that is, plants remain in their grow pots and are placed inside a waterproof, decorative planter.

There are a number of advantages to double-potting instead of direct potting. First, such plants are easy to install or take out and replace, with a minimum of mess and effort. Just lift out the pot and you're done. In contrast, direct-planting involves more work. You need to remove the entire root ball and most of the soil medium, wrap up the root ball or jam it into an empty grow pot, remove any remaining soil in the container and replace it with fresh soil, take the new plant out of the grow pot and place it into the decorative container, adjusting its height as needed, then fill in around the sides with fresh medium, and clean up the mess you've just created.

A second advantage is that it is much easier to control and correct the watering of plants, especially if a plant is overwatered by mistake. If a plant is double-potted and is sitting in water, a kitchen baster or portable siphon pump can be used to remove the excess water. If a direct-planted container is overwatered, it must be taken outdoors or to a slop sink and tilted on its side to drain off any excess water. But even that may not be enough to correct the problem and keep the plant from developing root rot.

A third benefit of double-potting is that containers can easily be changed out if there is a design change in the space, or for special occasions. It's easy to remove the outside container of a double-potted plant and replace it with a new one. With a direct-planted one, you need to remove the bare-root plant, replace soil medium, and go through the same steps you would if changing out the plant.

A final advantage of double potting is that if a number of different plants are in the same decorative container, such as in a color bowl, each individual plant can be watered according to its specific needs, rather than watering all of the plants uniformly, even if their needs are quite different. In a direct-planted container, all the plants receive about the same amount of water. If all the plants are still in their individual grow pots, each pot can be watered as needed.

Mechanics of Double-potting a Plant

When double-potting a plant, the goal is to hide the grow pot and any other mechanics so the plant looks like it's direct-planted, even though it is not. Not only does this result in a more attractive look, it also helps to deter anyone from trying to pull the plant out and steal it (the nicest places usually have the most trouble with plant theft).

The decorative container needs to be slightly wider and taller than the grow pot. Fortunately, most containers made specifically for plants are designed for the standard grow pot sizes. The planter should be about 2 to 3 inches taller than the grow pot and 2 to 3 inches wider at the top diameter. For example, a plant in a 14-inch grow pot should be placed into a 16- or 17-inch diameter planter. Note that if the planter is much larger than the grow pot, it will be much more difficult to hide the grow pot and other mechanics. If it is too small, the grow pot may show above the rim of the planter and may not fit all the way down into the planter, looking awkward and perhaps becoming top-heavy.

Table 5. Grow pots and recommended planter sizes.

Grow pots			Planter size (inches)
Pot size (inches)	Width × height (inches overall)	Weight (pounds)	
6	6½ × 6	3	7½–8
6 azalea	6½ × 5	3	7½–8
7	7 × 6	4	8–9
8	8 × 7	5	9
9	9 × 8	9	10–11
10	10 × 9½	13	12–13
11	11 × 10½	20	12–14
12	12 × 11	25	14–15
14	13¼ × 12	35	16–17
17	17 × 15	75	19
21	21 × 18	200	23
21	21 × 24	300	23
28	28 × 21	450	30

SOURCES: Data on grow pots from Florida Nursery, Growers and Landscape Association. Planter size recommendations based on the author's experience.

Staging Materials and Top Dressings

Since the grow pot is a couple of inches smaller in diameter than the planter, staging material must be placed in the gap between the two. This material allows top dressing to be used to hide the rim of the grow pot.

Foam strips or foam collars are the usual staging materials. This high-density, flexible material stays in place thanks to the pressure created between the pot and planter. The foam strips are usually 2 to 3 inches in width and height, and some made specifically for plants may include adhesive on one side to keep the collar connected to the planter. These foam strips are readily available through interior plantscape suppliers. Similar foam strips used for insulation can be found at hardware and home improvement stores.

If the planter is a little too large, the foam will slip down and will not stay in place. If the difference is very slight, the problem can be remedied by doubling up on the foam collar, using a wider width of foam, or applying an adhesive.

With the exception of 4-inch plants, decorative planters should be several inches deeper than the height of the grow pot. This creates a space for risers to raise the grow pot off the floor of the planter. Excess water can then drain out of the grow pot after it's been watered and the water will collect at the bottom of the decorative container, where it eventually evaporates. Using risers

Foam strips adhere to the side of the decorative planter and fill the space between the grow pot and planter. Moss or another top dressing can then be added to hide the mechanics and make the plant look like it is direct-planted in the decorative container.

prevents plants from sitting in water for long periods and developing root rot. Risers also make it easier to apply a thinner layer of top dressing so the watering needs of a plant can more easily be monitored. If a plant is too deep into the planter, a thicker layer of top dressing would be needed and could interfere with watering needs.

Risers can be made out of any number of materials. They raise up the grow pot in the decorative container to provide drainage and eliminate the need for excessive amounts of top dressing. Blocks of Styrofoam are frequently used to raise up a plant. Grids made out of rigid plastic can be purchased from companies that carry interior plantscape supplies. Some companies use "donuts" cut from wide PVC pipe, and pipe suppliers will often cut the pipe into donut rings for a reasonable fee. Bricks and gravel are rarely used due to their weight. However, if theft is a problem, using a heavier-weight material can often deter thieves from stealing plants.

Paper and cardboard should never be used as collars or risers. They will disintegrate and collapse when they get wet, and eventually start to mildew and smell. Cockroaches, mice, and other critters love to eat paper and may make their homes in planters, something clients do not want to happen.

Risers and foam collars are rarely used with small 4-inch plants such as orchids. These may come already planted in decorative containers, or fit tightly into a planter that is just slightly larger than the grow pot. Overwatering is usually not a problem since these plants dry out faster due to the smaller volume of soil medium.

Top dressings are used as mulch to hide the rim of the grow pot and staging materials. They give a finished, professional look to plants in decorative containers. In some cases the top dressings add interest and can "upgrade" the look of the design, making the plants and containers look more expensive and luxurious.

In the 1960s and 1970s, pine bark nuggets were

the preferred staging material for both potted plants and indoor atrium gardens. The nuggets were cheap and plentiful and gave plants a natural, outdoor look. However, as companies gained more experience working with indoor plants they discovered that cockroaches were attracted to the bark, eating the wood and hiding in between the chips. In addition, fungus gnats were also attracted to the bark-covered soil which stayed moist and created the perfect breeding grounds with rich, slowly-decaying organic matter. Most companies stopped using pine bark chips, although a few companies today will use shredded cedar for atriums since it decays much more slowly and does not attract insects as much as pine bark.

Spanish moss was also a favorite top dressing at one time, but many companies found that it didn't stay looking fresh for very long, deteriorating and changing to a dark, dingy gray within a few months. Today most professionals use wood excelsior that has been shredded and dyed to look much like Spanish moss. It is more sustainable and lasts longer than Spanish moss.

Polished or unpolished river rock is used occasionally as a top dressing on potted plants. It has a more upscale look than wood excelsior moss, but is heavy and shipping costs can be very high. The weight also makes delivery and installation more difficult and time-consuming. The rocks can be difficult to keep clean looking, becoming dirty over time and discolored from hard water deposits.

Today poly pebbles are used frequently for top dressing, resembling river rock but made from lightweight recycled plastics. They are less expensive to ship and much easier to install, although they also need to be cleaned occasionally.

Green sheet moss and green club moss can give a very classy, fresh look to potted plants. Materials

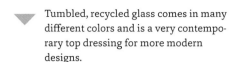

Tumbled, recycled glass comes in many different colors and is a very contemporary top dressing for more modern designs.

can be expensive, especially club moss, and over time they will become discolored and need to be replaced. They can, however, make a design look luxurious. Mosses are often used for color bowls and orchids.

A relatively new top dressing for plants is recycled glass, available in a large variety of colors and more commonly used in many European countries, as well as Australia and New Zealand. The glass, which has been tumbled to remove any sharp edges, is quite safe to use. It's available through plantscape suppliers as well as from companies that recycle glass products. This material gives a very modern, clean look to a design and so may be out of place in more traditional plantings. Expect to see more tumbled glass used as this product becomes more familiar to the public. Replacing plants usually requires that the glass be replaced, too, although it can be screened, washed, and used again. Many designers use tumbled glass in the areas outside of the rim of the grow pots to make replacements easier and to keep the glass looking fresher for a longer time.

Many staging materials for indoor plants are eco-friendly. Wood excelsior fiber moss is a sustainable by-product of the lumber industry. Poly pebbles, risers, and foam strips and collars can be found that are made from recycled plastics. Tumbled crushed glass is made from recycled glass and is available in a wide variety of colors. All of these options help make indoor plants more "green."

Other materials for top dressings will no doubt continue to become available, gaining and waning in popularity along with design trends. The purposes remain the same—hide the grow pot and mechanics, give a finished look to the design, deter theft, and make the plant look like it is planted directly into the planter.

DECORATIVE CONTAINERS

In many designs, the choice of decorative containers has more impact than the choice of plants. And never before have there been so many choices in shapes, colors, and finishes, everything from plastic cylinders, to wood urns, to fiberglass egg-shaped bowls. The choice of containers will set the mood and tie the entire design of the space together, so choose wisely.

Decorative containers hide the plastic grow pot and provide a well for water drainage. The dimensions must be appropriate for the height and diameter of the grow pot so it will slip in easily. Decorative containers must also be waterproof to protect floors and furniture from water damage. Most containers made specifically for indoor plants are already sealed and waterproofed. However, if you are using found objects, older planters, or custom-designed containers, they may need to be waterproofed. This can be done by using a watertight sealant on the interior of the container, both the bottom and sides. Waterproof liners are also available and can be used with most decorative containers.

One Style + One Color = One Cohesive Design

You may also hear decorative containers called cache pots or planters. Cache pots refer back to Victorian times and bring to mind fancy, ornate, porcelain or brass containers which are rarely, if ever, used today. Planters usually refer to rectangular or square containers that hold more than one plant. They are often made of wood, metal, plastic, or fiberglass and are used most often outdoors or in large atriums.

For a professional, pulled-together design, choose one style and one color of container for all of the plants in the space, particularly the floor plants. Sometimes you may need to choose a different shape for tabletop plants due to the dimensions and the amount of space available. If so, be sure the shape complements the other

Although two styles or shapes of white planters are used in this design, they work together because they are the same color and finish. The cobalt blue pyramids also have the same finish and are made of the same material as the decorative white containers, although they have a different shape and color. They complete the look because they complement the silver and blue specks in the floor tile and other fixtures in the space.

containers and is the same color (or within the same color palette).

Unless done carefully, mixing shapes or colors can make a space look junky, as though each plant were purchased at a separate time and haphazardly added to the collection. It does not reflect a well-thought-out plan and purposeful design, and should be avoided. If you must incorporate existing containers into your design (as for a residential client with a sentimental attachment to a particular container,) then choose the new containers to complement the existing ones.

Materials

Decorative plant containers come in a number of materials, each with a specific look. Some containers are eco-friendly and made with recycled materials or sustainable products. Colors, finishes, and prices are dependent on the material used to manufacture the container. The price for containers can also vary widely and many containers may cost more than the plants themselves.

These handsome containers are made from more than 80 percent post-consumer recycled plastic and are eco-friendly as well as budget-friendly.

PLASTIC

Plastic decorative containers tend to be the least expensive choice and are used most frequently in designs where the budget is limited. Most plastic containers come in simple cylinder shapes with no lip on the top and with a matte or gloss finish. They are available in various colors, including neutrals, metallic, and bright neon tones. These plastic decorative containers are already waterproof and many include a raised center to lift the plant out of any drainage water that accumulates. The containers are lightweight and are often designed to stack together, saving on shipping costs. Plastic containers are usually used in moderately priced homes, small offices and businesses, and casual restaurants.

FIBERGLASS

A wide variety of fiberglass containers are available in an almost unlimited number of shapes and colors. Fiberglass molds are easily made and can be an excellent choice for custom design work. Due to the nature of the material, it can also be used to make organic shapes and bowls. A lip on the top of the container adds a nice touch and helps a container to look more high-end.

Fiberglass containers are usually made with a glossy or textured finish. They can mimic the look of wood, stone, iron, seashells, rock, or nearly anything else imaginable. They are waterproof and may or may not have a raised center for drainage. Some brands of fiberglass containers include their own subirrigation system to make watering easier.

Some fiberglass containers may require a moderate lead time for manufacturing, especially if you are ordering a custom design or color. Fiberglass is relatively lightweight and is usually shipped with each container in its own package to protect the finish. Multiple containers may be shipped on a palette to lower the costs of handling the individual packages.

Unusually shaped fiberglass containers such as this cross-shaped one may require some lead time to manufacture, so be sure to order early.

Standard-shaped containers such as cylinders, Italian rim, and oriental bowls are often readily available from manufacturers in a variety of standard colors.

Fiberglass containers can fit into almost any décor and are used for projects with moderate to high-end budgets. Unusual shapes and finishes may increase the price, while standard shapes and colors will fit most commercial project budgets.

CERAMIC AND TERRA COTTA

Containers made of ceramic or terra cotta are rarely used in commercial settings for several reasons. Their look is much more casual and does not fit into most contemporary and modern designs, although they are still found in Southwest-themed designs, Victorian gardens, and very casual designs. They are heavy, and chip and break easily. Furthermore, they can be difficult and costly to ship and are not water proof. Most ceramic and terra cotta containers that are used are made locally or sold to home owners.

METAL

Metal containers are once again gaining in popularity. Metal cylinder containers were popular in the 1970s and 1980s, but fell out of favor for a number of reasons. Often they were heavy and expensive, and developed water leaks at the seams. Those with a polished finish scratched easily, and all of them corroded over time. They often gave the interior a cold, industrial look that became outdated in the 1990s and 2000s.

Now metal containers, and those with a metal finish, are once again becoming popular, especially in more minimalist and modern designs, but the shapes have changed dramatically. Modern metal containers are available in urn shapes, rectangles and squares, ovals, curved planters, saucer-shaped bowls, and many others.

Ceramic and terra cotta pots are not often used today. In Victorian indoor gardens, such as this one at a conservatory, they add old-world charm to a variety of lush, flowering plants.

Made from brushed steel, these planters project a very modern, industrial look. They include a plastic insert.

Looking like rustic metal, this rectangular planter is actually fabricated from fiberglass. The finish, which is molded into the fiberglass, makes the product durable and scratch-resistant.

Polished aluminum has been replaced with brushed metal, bronze, and cast-iron look-alikes in shiny, matte, and textured finishes. Gem tones and neon-bright colors will also become more available as these hues become more popular in the interior design.

WOOD PLANTERS

Until recently, wood planters were rarely used indoors. They were typically handmade, white-painted box planters for larger trees in shopping malls and atriums, similar to those made for outdoor use, and they imparted an English cottage garden image which was popular in the 1970s and 1980s. These wooden planters were not waterproofed, and so a metal or plastic liner had to be installed if they were used indoors.

Today most wood planters are made from rapidly renewable woods or bark. They are a smart choice when a natural-looking decorative container is needed.

A few manufacturers are making high-end decorative containers from bamboo and other sustainable products. Some use the bark of sustainable trees such as abaca (a relative of the banana tree), pressed onto a durable shell and finished with multiple layers of glossy resin. The high-gloss finish shows off the natural ribbons of color and are quite beautiful. These containers are often shaped into urns or other modern shapes. The darker wood colors give a very rich look and fit best in traditional settings, and in settings with darker-colored furnishings. Lighter-colored woods such as bamboo may be used in more contemporary designs.

These modern wood containers are made by pressing natural bark from the abaca tree onto a durable synthetic shell, then covering it with many layers of clear resin.

Texture transforms a copper planter into a contemporary piece of art.

OTHER MATERIALS

Other materials are sometimes incorporated into plant containers and sold for interior use. Seashells are sliced and strategically fitted and glued onto a synthetic base, giving a high-textured look popular at seaside homes and resorts. Stone powder may be mixed with resin and backed with fiberglass, looking like marble or stone but weighing much less. These stone powder containers may also be used outdoors to coordinate with the exterior of the building.

No matter what the material, the type of finish has a direct effect on the perceived value of a container. A matte finish tends to look more casual and less expensive. A high-gloss finish gives the impression of an expensive, modern and high-end design. A highly textured finish lends a more organic, contemporary or eco-friendly look.

Tapered cylinders are more modern-looking then straight-edged cylinders, especially in metallic or high gloss finishes.

Fishbowl or Chinese-styled containers are usually used in more traditional settings.

Shapes

Along with the color and finish, the shape of a decorative plant container has a dramatic impact on the overall design of an interior space. With the advances in fiberglass containers, almost any shape is possible.

CYLINDER

Straight cylinder decorative containers have been used in the interiorscape since the 1960s, perhaps even earlier than that. They fit more traditional settings and establish a feeling of stability. Often they blend in with the other décor and rarely stand out as a major design feature. They can tend to look outdated and inexpensive, especially in plastic or polished metal finishes. They are often used in building lobbies, conservative businesses, and lower-budget designs.

Today's cylinder containers are usually tapered at the bottom. They may also include fluting or other textures. These variations set them apart from older models and give a more contemporary, upgraded look while still keeping within the budget.

FISHBOWL

Fishbowl containers are narrower at the top and taper out about a third of the way down. They are similar in shape to porcelain Chinese fishbowl containers that are still popular in certain parts of the world. Most fishbowl shapes are made in fiberglass and have a distinctive lip on the top edge. These containers have a modestly more expensive look while blending into the background of a design, especially in neutral colors. Not used as often in today's designs, these traditional containers can be found in higher end lobbies, offices, and private homes.

URNS

Urns are vertical planters that are taller than they are wide, tapering at the bottom and wider at the top. They can be 4-sided or rounded. This suits a modern look and is used often in today's designs. Most are made from fiberglass and come in many different colors and finishes. Vertical urns are used to direct traffic flow, act as room dividers, and provide height where it is needed in the design.

Urn-shaped containers create height with a relatively small footprint. They can be used instead of a large towering plant when height is needed, but floor space is limited. Urns range in height from 2 feet to 6 feet tall or more. Any size plant can be used, including short vines such as pothos, or tall vertical plants such as rhapis palms or marginata canes. Such plants are a great option when tall plants would be too wide or are too expensive to use.

Urns can be found in almost any type of interior space, including building lobbies, offices,

 Taller than wide and tapering at the bottom, this planter combines an organic shape with the vertical lines of an urn.

hospitals, restaurants, hotels, and high-end residences. They give the space a modern, contemporary, sophisticated look while keeping within the budget.

BOWLS

Bowls are low, saucer-shaped containers used most frequently on desktops and tabletops. Such containers are often designed to accommodate several smaller plants grouped together, all in the same bowl, for greater impact. Plants may be all of the same type or a mix of foliage plants or colorful blooming plants.

When a bowl has several colorful flowering plants in it, it may be referred to as a "color bowl." Note that the word *color* refers to the flowers, not to the decorative container itself.

Most bowls are made from fiberglass or metal and are generally employed in office reception areas or on the top of filing cabinets. Occasionally larger bowls are utilized on the floor, typically with a taller plant in the middle surrounded by smaller vining or flowering plants in the same bowl.

Since bowls are shallow, the size of plants that can be used is limited by grow pot height and root ball depth. Six-inch plants are most common in bowls. The rims of the grow pots may stick up above the rim of the bowl, in which case the plants may need to be mounded and covered with a top dressing to hide the tops of the grow pots.

- Bowls are not always round. They may also be rectangular or organic in shape.

- If used on the floor, bowls may be placed on metal stands to raise them up for higher visibility and design impact.

- Some organic-shaped containers feature small planting holes at the top, creating interesting planting designs for desktops and reception desks.

ORGANIC SHAPES

Organic-shaped containers are the newest trend in the interiorscape. They are characterized by soft curves and often asymmetrical shapes. There are no hard corners or edges on organic-shaped containers. Often they are works of art unto themselves. Many organic shapes are used as planter bowls for desks and tabletops, but larger containers are also available. The lip on the top of these containers may cover the entire top except for a few holes in which to set the plants.

Organic-shaped containers give the space a comfortable, very contemporary look and help guests feel relaxed. Designers use such containers to convey a sense of eco-friendly surroundings or being attuned to nature. Organic shapes are frequently used in spas and classy hotels and restaurants. More modern and eco-friendly businesses and homes also use organic shapes.

OTHER SHAPES

In addition, other novelty-shaped containers are available for more modern, contemporary designs. Most are made from fiberglass and may need to be ordered in advance. They may also feature unusual textures or patterns and come in a variety of finishes.

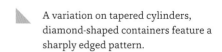 A variation on tapered cylinders, diamond-shaped containers feature a sharply edged pattern.

 Urns and cylinders that are tapered at both the top and bottom work well with mid-century and retro designs.

 Round, globe-shaped decorative containers can soften the look of an industrial design and add a contemporary feel.

 Triangle-shaped containers must be placed in metal stands to remain upright.

Metal plant stands provide an upgraded look, especially when used with tall urns or cylinders.

Plant stands may also be made from other materials, such as fiberglass, in a variety of shapes.

Fiberglass balls, pyramids, and other shapes look best in groups of plants when the finish is the same as that of the decorative planters. Different colors may be used to complement other design elements in the space.

Accessories

Depending on the needs of the space, accessories are sometimes added to containers. Decorative containers may be put on casters or a rolling tray if a client frequently needs to change the location and arrangement of plants. For example, a hotel may need to move plants around in their ballroom for various functions, such as weddings and corporate events. Adding casters allows the client to move plants freely without worrying about tilting the containers, spilling top dressing and soil, or damaging the plants.

Plant stands can provide additional height for plants without requiring all-new containers. Most plant stands today are made of metal rods in the shape of a rectangle or triangle. They look very modern and sleek, unlike the wooden plant stands that are sold for home use. Plant stands may also be made from other materials, such as fiberglass, in various forms.

Fiberglass pyramids, balls and other shapes work well with groupings of plants when they are in the same finish as the decorative containers. They can break up the monotony of a larger grouping of plants and add interest to the overall design.

Indoor gardens create a parklike setting
for people to meet and relax.

Interior Gardens

In the 1970s and 1980s, many buildings were designed with atrium areas specifically for indoor gardens. Today's interior gardens have a more modern look, while still fulfilling many purposes in the overall design and function of atriums and lobbies.

For the intents of this book, an interior garden is defined as a grouping or mass of plants that are planted in a substrate with the appearance of being planted in the ground. Plants may or may not be in their individual grow pots, but they appear to be direct-planted in the substrate or soil medium. Individual plants in decorative containers may be incorporated into the garden as focal points, but do not comprise the majority of the planting space. Other decorative elements such as rocks, pathways, garden furniture, sculpture, and water features may be included.

Indoor gardens provide a number of benefits to the building's tenants and visitors, besides the overall health and well-being benefits of indoor plants in general. A well-designed interior garden may function in all or some of the following ways:

AS AN INFORMAL PLACE FOR GUESTS AND VISITORS TO MEET. People are innately drawn to gardens and have an instinctive tendency to want to meet and talk with each other in natural surroundings. If you wish to encourage people to use your garden as a place to meet, provide seating.

AS A PLACE FOR RELAXATION AND RESPITE. Indoor gardens are often included in the lobbies of hospitals for patients and their visitors, providing a quiet place to escape hospital activity and get some much-needed rest.

As a collaboration space for business meetings. If you are designing a garden for business meetings, provide tables and seating.

As a beautiful venue for special occasions, such as weddings and corporate functions. Atrium gardens in hotels and special events centers provide a timeless backdrop for formal ceremonies and photographs.

As a dining area. Lobby restaurants and specialized theme restaurants may incorporate garden spaces and plants. People are more likely to stop and eat in an interior garden with a parklike setting. To encourage this use, provide comfortable tables and chairs for formal dining, or casual benches for guests to enjoy a quick snack or meal.

As an educational site. Indoor gardens provide many opportunities for children to learn about the natural sciences. Signage and planned activities add impact to the lessons learned.

As a spot for growing food and herbs for urban gardens. With plenty of sunlight, indoor gardens can provide fresh herbs, fruits, and vegetables for a restaurant or community garden where outdoor space may be limited.

As a setting for creative thinking. Indoor gardens provide a space for everyone from engineers to artists to take a break, relax, and allow their creativity to come to the forefront.

To reinforce the building's earth-friendly marketing brand. An indoor garden visually shows that the building's owner is concerned about the environment, by bringing a piece of it indoors.

To raise humidity to more comfortable levels and increase oxygen levels. Gardens can make the indoor environment more physically comfortable, especially when green walls and water features are included. Indoor gardens are especially useful for this purpose in arid climates, such as Las Vegas and other desert cities.

An interior garden sends a message to visitors. It implies that whoever owns the building or manages it care about those who come to the garden. Gardens are, by their nature, nurturing, relaxed, and comfortable settings, whether they are indoors or outdoors.

DESIGN PRINCIPLES

When designing an interior garden, use the same design principles as for container plantings or outdoor gardens. Incorporate symmetry, balance, proportion, scale, and color harmony, keeping in mind that the design may have a 360-degree view, as opposed to container plantings that may be against walls and windows.

A garden should look balanced when viewed from directly above. It may be symmetrical in design, such as a formal indoor garden in a public conservatory, or asymmetrical as are most contemporary indoor gardens in commercial spaces. If, for example, all the larger plants are placed on one end of the garden, it will appear to be leaning or sliding to that end of the floor. An unbalanced design may make the entire space look like it's sinking, a very disturbing effect for people walking through the area. Spacing larger plants at carefully designed intervals will create interest and focal points throughout the garden, adding to the sense of calm and relaxation.

The size of the garden should be in proportion to the overall size of the space. A small island garden in a large atrium will appear lost and out of place, whereas a large garden will make a smaller space seem overcrowded and overgrown. The height of the plants used should also be in proportion to the space and height of the ceiling. In general, the tallest plants should be no more than two thirds the height of the ceiling in a larger space. The bottom of the canopy should be above head level if people will be walking underneath or close to taller trees and plants.

Plants used in the interior garden should be harmonious in color to each other, as well as to the décor of the rest of the space design. A brightly colored children's museum calls for strong, bright colors of leaves and flowers in the garden. A subdued theme in a hospital atrium dictates muted greens, silvers, and pastel-colored flowers in the interior garden.

The colors of the plants should complement each other—brightly colored crotons with their red, yellow, and orange variegated foliage will look out of place next to *Aglaonema* 'Silver Queen' and soft pink begonias, but crotons will work beautifully with brightly colored bromeliads and pothos.

The amount of floor space available for an interior garden will have the largest impact on your design. On the one hand, the garden may only be 100 square feet or less, more of an island planting than one of any stature. On the other hand, the garden may be quite expansive, perhaps several acres or the size of several American football fields. In such cases the interior garden will most resemble an outdoor garden space, and the design will be that much more important to its overall impact.

Another consideration is whether people will be able to walk through the garden, or will only view it from the edges. If people will be walking through, then the view must be interesting not only from the edge of the garden but also from the interior facing out. Pathways and clearly marked entrances and exits will also need to be provided.

The larger the garden space, the more important it becomes to use floor plans and architectural drawings to design the garden space.

The soft white, cream, silver, and pink color combination found in this small garden planting complements the pastel tones of the tile floor.

DRAWING UP PLANS

When designing an interior garden, it greatly helps to draw out the space and design, whether by hand or using a computer software program. In addition to CAD, there are many software packages available to design gardens for the home or commercial spaces that can be modified for designing interior gardens. Simply choose the provided plant symbols to represent your indoor plant choices and make notes as to the indoor plants these will represent in your design. For beds of the same plant, draw the outline of the entire bed and mark small x's to indicate the placement of individual plants.

The designs should be drawn from a bird's-eye view, looking from directly above the garden, just as floor plans are used to indicate the placement of containerized plants. The architect or designer may have already indicated the outline of the garden space, especially if it is being constructed at the same time as the rest of the building, or they may have left this part of the project to the interior plant contractor to design and construct.

The garden should be placed in an area where it can be enjoyed without impeding the traffic flow of people walking through the space. It is very helpful to draw in the traffic flow first, along with other design elements and furnishings. Keep in mind that once an indoor garden is placed, it will be very costly to re-position the garden, especially if any digging or concrete work is involved (and it usually is).

Depending on the size and use of the space, an indoor garden may be placed against a wall or bank of windows, in the center of the floor, or off-centered on the floor. If the garden is centered or off-centered on the floor, the designer will need to determine if the intent is for people to walk around the garden and/or through the garden.

An indoor garden will look most appealing if its outer edges are curved and the overall outline as seen from above is organic in nature. Hard, straight edges look very formal, stark, and uninviting. Straight edges in a garden say "Keep out," not "Come and enjoy."

The only time to use straight edges is if you are designing a planter box–styled garden, or using a straight-edged garden as a border for another focal point in the space (rather than the garden itself being the focal point of the space). Most often one type of plant is used, or perhaps one taller hedge-like plant with a border of blooming plants.

When designing a garden, first mark the traffic flow pattern and then the overall outline for the garden space on the floor plan. Keep in mind that edges that curve inward draw people into the curve, and edges that curve outward direct people along the outer edge of the curve. Both are necessary in the design. The apex of inward curves is a good place for entryways, benches, and focal points.

The edge of a garden must also be bordered in some way to prevent people from walking into the plants and destroying them. This can best be done with edging material, a stone border, or a short wall. A border will also prevent soil and mulch from washing out onto the floor when the garden is watered.

Next, draw in the placement of any focal point(s). Larger gardens may have more than one focal point, in which case there should be a main focal point for the entire garden space, with subordinate focal points in strategic spaces, each leading the eye to the central focal point.

The focal point may be a specimen plant, sculpture, water feature, or other design element.

Larger gardens are often designed for people to walk through and may include a sidewalk or pathway for pedestrians.

A tall or unusual specimen plant works well as a focal point in any garden design. A piece of sculpture used as a focal point helps set the tone, whether it is contemporary in design or traditional. A water fountain, waterfall, or circulating pond attracts attention not only visually but also with its sounds of water splashing and moving around. A seating area can be a focal point, drawing people in to sit and relax for a while. Structures and props such as a small greenhouse or seasonal display are delightful discoveries while walking through an interior garden.

Once the focal point(s) have been determined, the rest of the planting areas can be drawn in place, leading to the focal points and complementing the overall design. Think in terms of massing plants in beds rather than a single plant here and there. A bed of pothos vines, for example, can be used to border a pathway or the outer edge of a garden. A mass of flowering mums adds color and charm. A group of arboricola bushes provides a visual pathway leading to a towering specimen ficus tree.

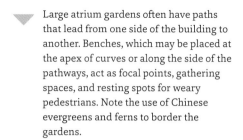

Large atrium gardens often have paths that lead from one side of the building to another. Benches, which may be placed at the apex of curves or along the side of the pathways, act as focal points, gathering spaces, and resting spots for weary pedestrians. Note the use of Chinese evergreens and ferns to border the gardens.

The focal point in this small garden is determined by height. The large adonidia palm (*Adonidia merrillii*) is the primary focal point. Then, attention is drawn to the mid-level anthuriums as a secondary focal point. Finally, the brightly colored foliage plants act as a third and final focal point, bringing the eye to the edge of the planter box.

These beds and masses should each be of the same plant variety and size. They provide a blanket of color and a visual pathway to the focal points. The beds can be large or small, leading into other beds of other plants, each seamlessly flowing from one into the other. Beds and masses of plants can be repeated throughout the garden design, bringing a sense of unity and rhythm to the garden.

Shorter plants should be placed along the outer edges and pathways so people can see into the garden and feel more comfortable. Begin with groundcover plants and those that are below 18 inches tall, gradually moving to progressively taller plants towards the center of a planting area. The tallest plants should be in the center or rear of any planting area where they can be viewed and enjoyed from a distance, whether that means several feet or a hundred feet, depending on the overall size of the garden.

CREATING GARDEN ISLANDS

Larger interiorscapes essentially consist of islands or miniature gardens within a garden. Each area should have something in common with the other sections or islands—a plant variety, shape, color, or other design element repeated—and each area should flow smoothly into the next with adjacent borders.

Each island should have its own focal point, which should be subordinate to the major focal point for the entire garden. Also, each island should be limited in its plant palette in accordance with its size. Too many different plants will make the entire garden seem disjointed, haphazard, and without an overall design. By designing the garden on paper first, these potential problems can be eliminated.

Be sure to allow enough space between plants for growth, while using enough plants to provide a finished product from the very first day. Plants can always be cut back if they start to grow outside the design parameters.

Plants with more delicate leaves such as peace lily (*Spathiphyllum*) should be kept away from pathways and edges where they can easily be

Garden islands are created by using groupings of plant material. The weeping Buddhist pines are focal points for one island, while the fiddleleaf fig trees (*Ficus lyrata*) are focal points for another island. Some of the lower plants are repeated in both islands to create unity.

Bamboo plants line this peaceful walkway, growing in separate beds to maintain their size and to keep them from spreading.

damaged by passers-by. Likewise, plants with spines, pointed leaves, or leaves with sharp edges should be placed well away from the public or eliminated altogether as they pose a safety hazard. See Table 6 for some ideas on suitable garden island plants.

Bamboo plants, although quite striking, require a lot of sunshine and water to survive indoors. They have a very invasive root system and will quickly spread throughout an entire garden, even if they are kept in their grow pots. Bamboo should be kept in its own island or bed, where a forest or hedge of bamboo can be quite striking. If in a garden, it should be isolated from the rest of the plants with a wall that goes down to the bottom of the planter.

Table 6. Selected plants for indoor garden islands.

	Common name	Botanical name	Comments
Pathways and edges	Arboricola	*Schefflera arboricola*	6-inch pots
	Chinese evergreen	*Aglaonema* varieties	Compact forms in 6-inch pots
	English ivy	*Hedera helix*	—
	Heart-leaf philodendron	*Philodendron cordatum*	—
	Janet Craig Compacta dracaena	*Dracaena fragrans* 'Janet Craig Compacta'	—
	Pothos	*Epipremnum aureum*	—
	Snake plant	*Sansevieria* species	Compact forms
	Tricolor bromeliad	*Neoregelia* 'Tricolor'	—
Middle-ground massing	Arboricola	*Schefflera arboricola*	Bush form in 10-inch pots or larger
	Chinese evergreen	*Aglaonema* varieties	10-inch pots or larger
	Janet Craig dracaena	*Dracaena fragrans* 'Janet Craig'	Bush form
	Marginata	*Dracaena cincta*	Bush form
	Peace lily	*Spathiphyllum* hybrids	—
	Reflexa	*Dracaena reflexa*	—
	Striped dracaena	*Dracaena deremensis* 'Warneckii'	—
Focal points	Black olive tree	*Bucida buceras*	—
	Fiddleleaf fig	*Ficus lyrata*	Tree form
	Marginata	*Dracaena cincta*	As a specimen tree
	Ming aralia	*Polyscias fruticosa*	—
	Palms	various	Most tall forms
	Reflexa	*Dracaena reflexa*	As a specimen tree
	Sensation peace lily	*Spathiphyllum* 'Sensation'	—
	Weeping fig	*Ficus benjamina*	Tree form

INCORPORATING BLOOMING PLANTS

Incorporating blooming plants into a garden adds color, freshness, and the ability to change the appearance of the garden with the seasons or for special events. Most flowering plants will do well within a garden for anywhere from 10 days to 10 weeks or more, depending on the type of plant, amount of sunlight, temperature, and watering practices (see Table 7). Generally, blooming plants

A wide ledge built around the garden protects blooming plants that have been positioned so their flowers are away from the edge.

will hold up best in cooler temperatures (60 to 75 degrees Fahrenheit), bright indirect sunlight, and when kept slightly moist.

Due to the delicate nature of most flowers and the public's propensity to touch and pick them, blooming plants should be placed just beyond the reach of visitors. Yet, since they are usually shorter plants, they need to be visible from the edges and walkways. Using a small border of pothos or other vining plants just in front of flowering plants can solve the problem. Another solution is to build up a mound, with the blooming plants at the top, creating a stunning, beautiful focal point of color.

Since blooming plants may have different watering requirements than the rest of the garden, they should be kept in their individual grow pots in the interiorscape. This allows for easy replacement of plants when the time comes to change them out. A soil medium or ground cover can be used to cover the rims of the grow pots.

BUILDING THE GARDEN'S FOUNDATION

Building and planting an interior garden poses a number of issues, especially since most of the foundational structure is more or less permanent and cannot be changed without substantial cost and labor. Some interior gardens are bottomless and connect directly with the earth, requiring a good amount of digging. Others have a flat concrete base. Others may have a basement or garage underneath, making weight and the structural integrity of the building a priority.

Building the foundation for an interior garden is similar to building a planter box, but on a larger scale. It includes some type of floor or bottom, accommodations for drainage, walls, and a rim. Most of the structure will be below floor level.

Table 7. Selected blooming plants for interior gardens and their life expectancy.

Plant group	Life expectancy indoors
Geraniums	10 days
Tulips and daffodils	10 days
Azaleas	10 days to 3 weeks, longer in cooler temperatures
Easter lilies	1 to 2 weeks
Begonias	2 to 3 weeks
Chrysanthemums	2 to 4 weeks
Poinsettias	2 to 4 weeks
Kalanchoes	4 to 6 weeks
Bromeliads	8 to 12 weeks or more
Crotons*	4 to 12 months or more, depending on light

*Used for their colorful foliage instead of their flowers.

Due to design and construction restrictions, this garden could not be designed deep enough to hold the root ball of this 6-foot-tall bird of paradise plant (*Strelitzia nicolai*). The top dressing and pothos should be mounded to hide the grow pot of this large plant as much as possible.

Interior gardens can be raised and built up from the floor with a surrounding wall to increase the depth. Note how this planter has been covered with mirrors, reflecting back the design in the floor and creating interesting patterns and optical illusions.

First, the foundation of the garden must be deep enough to house the root ball of your largest plants. A garden that is just a few inches deep will only accommodate grass and moss—and not much else.

If your design calls for a 15-foot palm, assume the plant will be in a 21-inch diameter grow pot that is 24 inches in height. Plants need a minimum of 2 inches of top dressing to cover their grow pots. Large plants also need a minimum of 6 inches of additional soil substrate for root growth, and a minimum of 6″ of drainage material. This is an additional 14″ of substrate, in addition to the overall height of the grow pot or root ball.

In this example, the 15-foot palm needs to be buried to a depth of at least 32 inches to cover the rim of the grow pot (2 inches) and provide some room for the roots to grow (a minimum of 6 inches). Another 6 inches in depth is required for

drainage materials (gravel, soil separator, and pipe). This results in a planter depth of 4 feet for a tall plant in a 21-inch diameter grow pot.

Planters should be a minimum of 3 to 4 feet deep to accommodate most indoor plants. It may be possible to mound the soil substrate towards the center of the garden, but don't count on more than 24 inches of mounding to hold stable over any length of time.

Gardens can also be raised up from the floor, with a raised wall surrounding it. If the floor of the building is also the floor of the garden, you still need to provide the same minimum amount of depth, 3 to 4 feet. A garden with a 3-foot wall might work, but a garden whose soil surface is 4 feet in the air would not be practical.

When it is not possible to provide a depth of 3 to 4 feet for planters, plants are usually kept in their grow pots and do not exceed 7 feet in height. This reduces the needed planter depth to 19 inches. The overall height of the grow pots will be no more than 15 inches (as opposed to the standard 24 inches for taller plants) as no room for root growth is needed (6 inches saved), and drainage can be simplified with 2-inch risers instead of the usual 6 inches of drainage material and piping, with additional 2 inches of top dressing.

Staking may be needed for taller plants in gardens, especially when they are first planted, to provide stability until the root system has had a chance to grow outside the dimensions of the grow

This small atrium garden is being prepared for planting. Note that the garden has no bottom and extends directly into the soil.

pot and into the soil. This may require one to two years or more. In the traditional method of staking trees, heavy cable wire is wrapped around the trunk and secured to stakes in the ground, using three or four cables. Rubber hosing around the wires helps protect the bark or outer skin of these specimen plants until it is time to remove the stakes. A newer method is to wrap two or three heavy plastic ties around the tree trunk and attach the ends to tall stakes placed close to the trunk. This method is usually less expensive, exerts less pressure, and does not damage the tree.

DIRECT-PLANTING VS. DOUBLE-POTTING

When designing and installing an interior garden, the designer must answer the question, "Should the plants be taken out of their grow pots and direct-planted, or should they be left in their grow pots and double-potted?" The answer is yes to both options, depending on the plants and the garden itself.

In this garden, the foliage plants have been direct-planted into the container medium, while the flowering plants have been triple-potted to make replacement faster and easier.

The waterproof liner must be fitted to the planter and should come up to just under the rim.

Large specimen plants that will be a permanent part of the garden usually do best when they are taken out of their grow pots and planted directly into the soil substrate. A heavier soil that includes sand will provide some heft to the soil to support the weight of the plants. If a specimen plant is in a wood crate, the wood material should be removed. If the root ball is wrapped in burlap, the burlap should be cut in several sections around the root ball once the plant is set in the garden and before any soil is added around the root ball. Leaving the burlap on the bottom of the root ball is fine, as it will deteriorate over time.

Direct-planting allows the roots to grow out into the soil substrate in the garden, providing added support for the specimen plant and giving it an opportunity to absorb all the water and nutrients it will need to thrive. Invasive species such as bamboo, which may spread throughout the garden if left unchecked, can be left in their grow pots, although they will eventually burst the grow pot and spread into the rest of the garden.

Smaller plants that are less than 6 feet tall and that may need to be replaced at some point are best left in their grow pots. This will provide for easy replacement as needed. Double-potting will also allow for different watering needs of the various plant species in a garden bed.

Triple-potting may be done for blooming plants and seasonal plants in gardens to make their frequent replacement easier. In this method, an empty grow pot or plastic pot that is one size larger than the plant's grow pot acts as a liner and is dug into place in the garden. The blooming plant is then placed inside this larger plastic pot, and the rim covered with top dressing. The blooming plant can easily be lifted out and a new plant placed when the time comes to replace it.

WATERPROOFING, DRAINAGE, AND IRRIGATION

The inside surfaces of an interior garden must be waterproofed to prevent leakage, spills, possible injuries, and property damage. Concrete is not waterproof—it's a porous material. The best way to waterproof a garden is to use a thick, waterproof membrane manufactured specifically for such purposes. Be careful that any seams overlap and are sealed. The membrane should come up to just under the lip of the garden's rim and should be at

The waterproof liner must be clamped and sealed to the sides of the garden planter, as shown in this diagram from No Sweat! Waterproof Liners.

Coir is shipped in condensed blocks. When water is added, the blocks expand 5 to 10 times their original size, absorbing a large amount of water. Once the coir is expanded, it can be used as part of the soil substrate or on its own.

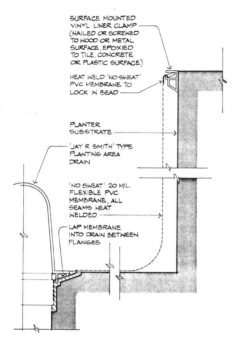

SURFACE MOUNTED VINYL LINER CLAMP (NAILED OR SCREWED TO WOOD OR METAL SURFACE, EPOXIED TO TILE, CONCRETE OR PLASTIC SURFACE)

HEAT WELD 'NO SWEAT' PVC MEMBRANE TO LOCK IN BEAD

PLANTER SUBSTRATE

'JAY R. SMITH' TYPE PLANTING AREA DRAIN

'NO SWEAT' 20 MIL. FLEXIBLE PVC MEMBRANE, ALL SEAMS HEAT WELDED

LAP MEMBRANE INTO DRAIN BETWEEN FLANGES

least 18 to 20 ml thick. Most liners are made from heavy-duty vinyl or flexible PVC. All seams should be watertight with a tensile strength of at least 70 percent.

Most of the time, no liquid sealers are needed. Many liquid sealants are petroleum-based or contain other chemicals that will eventually leach into the soil, possibly causing damage to plants. Prior to using any sealants, read the label carefully and consult with the manufacturer if there is any doubt about the chemicals in the sealant.

All interior gardens require a drainage system, and careful planning with the structural engineer and other building experts is worth the extra effort involved. Whether or not a garden is "bottomless" and goes straight into the ground, or has a hard base of cement or other building material, it needs a layer of drainage material at the bottom. Most often this is a layer of coarse gravel or similar materials. A horizontal-laying drainage pipe may also be needed depending on the circumstances, with vertical piping and a way to siphon out excess water for hard-based gardens. Any vertical pipe for siphoning should be capped and kept low to prevent any vandalism or any soil medium from clogging the pipe.

This drainage material should be a minimum of 6 inches deep to provide adequate drainage in most larger gardens. In the case of a garden that is not on the ground floor, it's best to consult with a building engineer and an architect to make sure the weight of the garden and its drainage material can be supported by the building structure.

Once the drainage material and piping are in place, they should be covered with a pervious membrane so water can drain down through the

membrane and out of the planter but the soil substrate cannot filter out and stays in place. A layer of substrate should then be added to the bed of the garden to the level of the bottom of the largest grow pot or root ball. The substrate should then be tamped down and watered and given some time to settle. Additional substrate and watering may be needed to bring the substrate to the proper level.

While installing the drainage material, a hose bib for a water source should also be added to the garden if possible. This will make watering the garden much easier and safer. Most hoses are 50 to 100 feet long, so provide enough hose bibs in the garden to reach all areas. An on/off valve with a locked cover plate is included with the hose bib. These can be opened with a universal water key and will keep vandals and mischief-makers from turning on the water and creating havoc.

In some larger gardens, an irrigation system may make more sense, using drip hose or water leaders in strategic areas. Some of the piping may need to be placed prior to the soil substrate. Concentrate first on providing water for the largest plants, then work your pattern to include other areas of the garden. Some hand watering by hose may still be needed, even if an automatic watering system is in place.

SOIL SUBSTRATES

A large portion of the garden's bed will be composed of some sort of substrate or filler material, usually referred to as the soil substrate. Remember that the roots of the larger plants—and many of the smaller plants, too—will be growing into the substrate. The substrate will most likely not include actual soil, as topsoil is usually too heavy for tropical plants and may include insects, disease-causing microbes, weed seeds, and other materials that no one wants indoors. The substrate should be sterile and made specifically for use with indoor plants.

A suitable substrate should contain peat, coir, or finely ground bark for water-holding and nutrient-holding capacity; coarse builder's sand for weight and drainage; and optional wetting agents, pH buffers, and/or time-released fertilizer as desired.

Mixtures that contain perlite, styrene pellets, or vermiculite are not recommended. These white particulates will eventually rise to the top of the substrate, drawing attention to themselves, looking unnatural, and taking away from the beauty of the garden.

Likewise, the garden is not the place to dump construction debris such as large chunks of concrete, rebar, and asphalt. These materials will not provide support or drainage, and over time chemicals from concrete and asphalt can leach into the soil and cause plant damage.

One brand of pre-mixed soil substrate specifically for indoor gardens is SuccessSoil. It contains coarse Canadian peat, coir, pine bark, cypress saw dust, coarse sand, and time-released fertilizer.

Coir is a fairly new product being used in the horticulture industry. Pronounced like "choir," this material is ground coconut fibers from the husk, which would normally be dumped by the coconut plantations. It does not decompose as quickly as peat or ground bark, is lightweight when dry, absorbs and holds a tremendous amount of water, and may contain ingredients that help to eliminate disease-causing microbes. Many growers are currently using coir for growing indoor tropical plants with good results. Some horticulturists are also finding that fungus gnats do not breed in coir, and it may deter other insects as well.

PLANTING

At this point the largest plants with the deepest root balls should be removed from their containers and placed in the garden. Fill in around the root balls with substrate until the level of the bottom of the next-in-size root balls are reached. Water and tamp as before, adding more substrate as necessary. Then set the intermediate-sized plants in place, usually keeping them in their grow pots. Repeat this process until the smallest plants have been placed and their grow pot rims covered with substrate or top dressing.

When all the plants are in place, the substrate should come up to the top of the waterproof membrane and be just a few inches below the rim of the garden's wall. Be sure the substrate is tamped down and that the grow pot rims are covered.

Eventually, substrates in gardens sink and seem to disappear, needing to be replenished from time to time as the garden matures. Where does it go? Some of it may filter out through tears in the pervious membrane into the drainage material. Some settles as the garden is watered, but most of it decays over time. Peat, coir, and finely ground bark are all organic materials that will decompose at different rates. Replenishing the substrate should be included in a maintenance budget to keep the garden looking fresh and healthy.

MULCHES, TOP DRESSINGS, AND GROUNDCOVERS

Most gardens will need some type of mulch, top dressing, or groundcover to complete the look, hide the mechanics, and cut down on the amount of water lost from the soil substrate through evaporation. Mulches usually refer to materials such as bark chips and shredded bark that are also used outdoors, while top dressings usually refer to materials used indoors. Groundcovers are live, low-growing plants used to cover the soil and unite the design.

In the past, bark mulch was widely used in atrium gardens. However, cockroaches and other insects were attracted to the bark and often made their permanent homes in the gardens. Shredded cedar mulch works better than pine bark and is less attractive to insects, although the light color may not work with all designs and may not fit into more contemporary settings.

Other top dressings do not have nearly as many problems as pine bark and can give a garden a more contemporary look. However, they may be more cost-prohibitive, so they are often used more sparingly in specific areas within a garden. These include tumbled glass, sheet moss, river rocks, and poly pebbles. Gravel and other pebble-sized rocks are also sometimes used, but their weight may be an issue and eventually they may become covered by soil substrate. Rocks of any size tend to be more labor-intensive and are not often used in indoor gardens as a top dressing.

Groundcovers used indoors are often taken out of their grow pots and planted directly into the soil substrate, since their purpose is to grow and cover the substrate. They may be used in front of taller plants, as edging along walkways and walls, or to fill in the space between plants. Since they frequently are far from the light source or shaded by the other plants, most groundcover plants are selected for their tolerance to low light levels. Their root system may be shallower due to their smaller size, so they may need to be watered more often than other plants in the garden. Examples of groundcovers include pothos (*Epipremnum aureum*), philodendron vines, English ivy (*Hedera helix*), and mosses.

PATHWAYS

When designing an interior garden, keep in mind that a horticulturist will need to walk through the garden and reach all of the plants to water and groom them on a regular basis. The best approach is to include a path or walkway for the horticulturist to use. This can be made from stepping stones, cypress bark, or gravel. To keep visitors out of the garden, keep the entryway to maintenance paths about 18 inches away from the edges, preferably hidden behind some plants or a decorative object.

If, on the other hand, you want visitors to walk through the garden, design a welcoming pathway of 24 to 36 inches wide. Safety is of the utmost concern. Use a cement pathway or closely spaced stepping stones. Well-packed cedar or gravel may also be used, but will be less stable and more difficult to walk on. The pathway will need to be maintained frequently, with any debris kept off the walkway. Watering the garden should be completed during off hours and pathways dry before the first visitor arrives. Safety cones may be used if the pathway is not dry, or if cleanup must be done during regular hours.

Edging should be used along walkways and the outside edges of any gardens that are floor-level. This will help to keep top dressing, plant debris, excess water, and soil substrate from wandering into walking areas. Edging materials used for outdoor gardens will work well indoors and may serve the dual purpose of keeping visitors out of the garden. The edging should be several inches taller than the level of the soil substrate.

Bowls filled with orchids and colorful
plants look perfect on a reception desk.

Color Bowls and Tabletop Gardens

8

The term "color bowl" refers to a low, round, bowl-shaped container with two or more flowering potted plants, arranged to look as if they are directly potted in the container. Color bowls are most often used on reception desks and coffee tables. They add color and a focal point to an indoor space. They can be used to attract visitors and guests to the receptionist or security desk for assistance. When budget is an issue, color bowls can be used as a substitute for cut floral arrangements, providing visual impact while lasting longer, thus costing less over time.

Large color bowls can be placed on the floor to direct attention and add color. For example, they can be placed near an elevator or doorway. Sometimes large color bowls are included in atrium gardens where they act as a focal point.

Color bowls are not intended to be permanent plantings. They may last from a couple of weeks to three or four months, depending on the plants that are chosen. To keep expenses under control, foliage plants may be added to help fill the bowl. On stricter budgets, plants with colorful foliage, such as crotons and caladiums, may be used instead of blooming plants, since these foliage plants will last three to six months or more.

Color bowls may also be used to celebrate special events and holidays, such as corporate functions, parties, and the Christmas season. Containers may be stored between events, or filled with small foliage plants when not in use as a color bowl.

During the year, this large color bowl is filled with flowering plants. Succulents or foliage plants fill in any empty space. At the holiday season, the same large color bowl is filled with holiday decorations, creating a miniature winter scene.

CHOOSING AN APPROPRIATE CONTAINER

Color bowls by their nature utilize shallow containers that are wider than they are tall. However, plants with their root balls must still fit into the bowl. Most blooming plants are grown in 6-inch-diameter pots that are also 6 inches in height (a 6-inch-high root ball), so the height of the container must be at least 6 inches tall

measured from the inside floor of the bowl. Some pots will need to be tilted to fit into the bowl, since the sides of the bowl are slanted and not perpendicular. To accommodate this tilt, a minimum height of 8 inches is recommended.

Low containers for color bowls are also available in modern, organic shapes. They tend to be less than 8 inches high, and may have more than one opening for planting. They are rarely used for displaying blooming plants, but are used for tabletop gardens instead.

Although two plants may be used, a minimum of three blooming plants will give maximum impact and a more rounded appearance. Allowing an extra couple of inches for tilting the grow pots, most color bowls need to be a minimum of 14 inches in diameter at the top of the bowl. Please note that the bottom of the bowl will most likely be smaller than this, generally by 2 to 6 inches, depending on the slant of the sides. Most bowl-shaped containers manufactured specifically for interior plantscape use begin at 14 inches in diameter and go up in size from there.

Color bowl containers come in many different colors and finishes. Most are neutral in color so they can fit into any décor. The shape can vary slightly, with some presenting a lower profile than others, although most are the traditional round bowl shape. Organic-shaped containers may make planting a bit tricky, and may require the use of smaller plants in 4- or 5-inch-diameter pots. If smaller plants are used, choose plants that are more tolerant of drying out, such as succulents and kalanchoes, to make caring for these color bowls easier.

As with containers for foliage plants, the color and finish of the bowl should complement the overall design of the space and should be of the

Most color bowls are in shallow, round containers with slanted sides. Plants often must be tilted slightly outward to fit into the container, such as the succulents in this orchid bowl.

same style, finish, and color as the other decorative containers used. If you are designing an interiorscape that will include both floor plants and color bowls, choose decorative containers that are also available in a bowl shape.

▼ Neutral-colored containers often work best for color bowls. The shape and color of the container should always complement the interior design of the space.

PLANTING COLOR BOWLS

Most color bowls are double-potted with the individual plants kept in their grow pots. This makes replacing plants fast and easy to do as their blooms start to fade. If the bowl is very shallow or an unusual shape, it may be necessary to take the plants out of their grow pots and plant them directly in the bowl, but this should be avoided whenever possible since there will be no drainage for excess water. When double-potted, the pots will be raised slightly off the floor of the bowl and tilted to fit into the decorative container, providing just enough space for drainage.

In most color bowls, there will be a gap between plants, especially along the bowl's edge. Plants should be turned within the bowl so their foliage overlaps and covers these gaps as much as possible. Still, some sort of top dressing will be needed, especially around the edges, to cover the gaps and hide the grow pots.

Color bowls are a great opportunity to use more unconventional and expensive top dressings, since they are relatively small containers yet very visible in the space. Green preserved sheet moss and club mosses make perfect top dressings, covering the grow pots and filling in the gaps while simplifying watering and plant replacement.

Sphagnum moss, Spanish moss, and moss-like wood excelsior products also work well. Wood excelsior moss is considered to be a more eco-friendly alternative to both Spanish moss, which grows outdoor on trees, and sphagnum moss, which is harvested from bogs. Excelsior moss is a by-product of the lumber industry and lasts much longer than natural mosses.

Top dressings such as tumbled glass, small pieces of polished river rock, or pea gravel will also work, but replacing plants will be more difficult. You may want to place these top dressings on a blanket of sheet moss to make replacements a little easier, or use them around the edges of the bowl only. Usually no other mechanics, such as foam strips, are used with color bowls due to lack of space.

Another option, especially on larger color bowls, is to use small filler plants instead of top dressing. These filler plants may be in 4- or 6-inch grow pots, depending on the size of the bowl. Recommended filler plants may include English ivy (*Hedera helix*), pothos (*Epipremnum aureum*), club moss (*Selaginella* varieties), low-growing

 Preserved sheet moss can be cut to size and used as a top dressing for color bowls and dish gardens.

 Dried sphagnum moss is sometimes used in color bowls and dish gardens. It can be a natural bleached color, or dyed green, red, or other colors.

▼ Fiberex, a brand of wood excelsior moss, is usually gray but can also be dyed green and other colors. It lasts much longer than sheet moss, sphagnum moss, or Spanish moss.

▼ Natural river rock can be used as a top dressing.

▼ Small white gravel chips are the perfect top dressing for this color bowl, complementing the white tabletop and décor.

agaves and other succulents, vining philodendron (*Philodendron cordatum*), and creeping fig (*Ficus pumila*). Vining plants should be kept trimmed off from the tabletop or floor for a neat, clean, professional look. These filler plants will most likely outlive the blooming plants and can be used many times over as new blooming plants are added.

Most color bowls will be viewed "in the round," from all sides and angles. Their design depends primarily on the number of plants being used. If only three plants are used, keep things simple and use three identical plants of the same variety, size, and color. A mass of one color will have more impact than a mix-and-match assortment of different plants. Use a top dressing instead of filler plants for smaller color bowls so the focus remains on the mass of color.

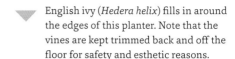

English ivy (*Hedera helix*) fills in around the edges of this planter. Note that the vines are kept trimmed back and off the floor for safety and esthetic reasons.

If four plants are used, place the tallest plant in the center, with the remaining plants tilted outwards around it. The center plant may be the same as the other three plants, or of a different color or variety, since it will be the focal point of the bowl. The taller plant may also be a foliage plant, such as a marginata or snake plant.

If the color bowl is placed against a wall and is meant to be viewed from one side only, the taller plant may be placed in the back instead, with the

Most color bowls are intended to be viewed from all angles. In this design, tall orchids are placed in the center, surrounded by shorter foliage plants.

Because this color bowl is placed in a corner and will not be viewed from behind, the tallest plants are planted in the center and towards the rear of the bowl. Dried stems have been added to give more height to this planting.

This large, opulent color bowl uses only two colors of flowering plants, with a variety of foliage plants acting as fillers.

lower plants arranged around it and in front. Filler plants may be used between the pots if space allows.

Recommended flowering plants for color bowls include chrysanthemums, bromeliads (for larger bowls), air plants (*Tillandsia* species), azaleas, kalanchoes, orchids, tulips and daffodils, and poinsettias. In fact, almost any type of flowering plant can be used. Bedding plants and other plants usually grown outdoors (including azaleas, tulips, and daffodils) will only last for a short time indoors, generally two weeks or less.

These arrangements can be used with nearly any size of color bowl and any number of plants. In larger color bowls with at least five plants, more than one variety of blooming plant may be used, alternating varieties. Foliage plants may be used as the alternating plant, too. Most times it's best to limit the flowering plants to two to three varieties and colors, with filler plants added as desired.

often found in urban gardens, patioscapes, and rooftop gardens. When used indoors, these plants will last one to two weeks and are only intended for short-term use, holidays, and special events. Among the plants suitable for an English garden color bowl are foxgloves, lupines, larkspurs, daffodils, tulips, chrysanthemums, marguerite daisies, and azaleas.

Orchid Bowls

Color bowls with orchids provide a luxurious, high-end look to the interiorscape. Orchid bowls are usually used on reception desks and coffee tables. Plants may be in 4- or 6-inch grow pots, and a top dressing is necessary to hide the pots. Orchids should always remain in their grow pots to provide enough support and protect roots. Often the decorative containers used for orchid bowls are smaller in size, less than the 14 inches in diameter usually recommended for color bowls.

All the orchids may be of the same color, height, and variety, creating a mass of blooms. Or, the colors of blooms may be mixed together to complement the décor of the space. Small accessories such as decorative rocks may be included in the design.

Usually orchid flower spikes need to be staked for support and to keep them vertical. The spikes can be tied to a piece of bamboo, a small branch, a piece of driftwood, or a green plant stake. Using raffia to gently secure the flower spike to the vertical support looks more natural and professional than most twist-ties or barrette-like orchid clips. If plant stakes are used, keep them close to the stems of the flower spike so they will not be too obvious.

English Garden Design

If an English garden or cottage theme is desired, the rules may be broken and several flowering plant varieties and colors may be mixed together. This arrangement may work quite well in a private residence or hotel with a traditional or Victorian décor, as well as public conservatories and formal gardens. However, this style rarely looks appropriate in a commercial office setting.

In an English garden design, each plant is different. The colors are also different but complement each other, often in pastel shades. The center plant is once again the tallest, surrounded by shorter plants. Ivies are frequently used as filler plants in this type of design.

Flowering plants used in this type of design are usually those intended for outdoor use. They are

▼ Orchid flower spikes are often tied to a small bamboo stake with raffia.

◀ With a few changes, any color bowl can be re-designed to celebrate the change in seasons or a special holiday.

Orchids in flower bowls may need to be watered weekly and should be watered with lukewarm water until water drains out of their grow pots. Most orchids are grown in bark nuggets or a potting medium with plenty of drainage, so most of the water will drain out and into the bottom of the orchid bowl. Any excess water should be drained out immediately to prevent root rot.

Remove any spent flowers to keep the orchids looking fresh. Flower spikes often continue to grow and produce new blooms for several months. Cut the flower spikes back to where they are green if they begin to brown.

Orchid bowls should last one to three months, depending on the variety used and the environmental conditions. Cool temperatures and indirect light, along with careful watering, will help to prolong their life and keep them looking beautiful for a long time.

Seasonal and Holiday Color Bowls

One of the advantages of including color bowls in an interior design is the ease of converting them into seasonal and holiday displays. Color bowls can be used to herald the arrival of spring, celebrate the autumn season, or welcome in the Christmas holidays by simply switching the blooming plants (see Table 8). In addition, accessories such as small branches can be added for more interest.

Table 8. Plants for seasonal displays.

Season	Plant materials	Notes
Spring	Azaleas	—
	Bird's nest fern	Use decorative miniature forms
	Daffodils	—
	Kalanchoes	Miniature forms with white, pink, or yellow flowers
	Pussy willow branches	—
	Tulips	—
	Weeping willow branches	—
Autumn	Chrysanthemums	—
	Fall foliage	Select branches with preserved leaves
	Kalanchoes	Red or orange flowers
	Pumpkins or gourds	Choose miniature sizes, real or artificial
Christmas holidays	Anthuriums	Select red forms
	Bromeliads	Red flowers
	Flocked branches	—
	Pine branches	—
	Poinsettias	—
	White birch branches	—

TABLETOP GARDENS

Tabletop gardens come in a variety of forms. They include dish gardens, miniature gardens, fairy gardens, and terrariums. The key to beautiful, long-lasting tabletop gardens is to choose plants that have the same light and watering requirements. Most of the time, the plants are taken out of their grow pots and planted directly into the tabletop container, so having the correct depth and providing adequate drainage is important.

Due to the size of these gardens, plants are usually smaller than those used in color bowls and other desktop containers. Typically they range from small plugs grown in the greenhouse to 2- or 4-inch grow pots. Thankfully, a wide variety of plants is available in these smaller sizes, including vines, mosses, and miniature flowering plants. Ornamental rocks, pebbles, figurines, and other accessories can add a touch of realism or whimsy, depending on the design.

Since most containers are shallow, a layer of drainage material is not needed. The container should be waterproof to avoid any water damage to the furnishings on which they will sit. To prevent root rot, care must be taken that these gardens are not overwatered.

To plant a tabletop garden, add a thin layer of a soil substrate with good drainage. Place the plants, then adjust for the height of the root ball so the root ball is below the rim of the decorative planter.

Containers used for tabletop gardens and dish gardens are usually smaller and shallower than those used for color bowls.

Add more potting medium to fill in the spaces between individual root balls.

One thing that tabletop gardens do not lack is interest. They are gaining in popularity with home owners and hobbyists, and will most likely become more popular in offices and commercial settings as this trend continues.

Dish Gardens

Dish gardens are a collection of small plants placed closely together in a low decorative container with little, if any, design to them. They are usually given as gifts and may wind up in the office space. Dish gardens differ from color bowls in that they contain mostly foliage plants and tend to be much smaller, less than 12 inches in length or diameter. Sometimes a decorative touch, such as a ribbon, twig, or ornamental animal may be added for additional interest.

The tallest plant is usually placed in the back with smaller plants arranged around it. Generally, each plant is a different variety. The plants may be direct-planted or kept in their grow pots with top dressing added as needed. Sometimes sand or small pea gravel is used as top dressing and may be glued together, forming a hard impenetrable mat on the surface, making watering almost impossible. This hard mat must be broken into pieces and lifted up temporarily to water these dish gardens. Sheets of dyed moss may also be used as a top dressing.

Watering dish gardens can be very tricky, especially if the containers are very low. There may be a lot of plants stuffed into a small amount of space, with root balls planted at or above the rim of the container. Water can run off the top dressing or soil medium without actually soaking the plants. Some containers may not be waterproofed and may damage the furniture on which they are sitting.

Dish gardens from the 1930s through the 1960s were traditionally planted in decorative ceramic containers. Newer, more contemporary styles may be planted in decorative plastic, fiberglass, or other types of containers. Unless well designed with an upgraded, modern container, dish gardens have a tendency to look cheap and old-fashioned. They are not usually used in a commercial setting.

▼ Modern dish gardens are planted in contemporary decorative containers and include several different varieties of plants. Twigs and other ornaments may be added for extra height and interest.

Miniature and Fairy Gardens

Miniature gardens and fairy gardens are similar to dish gardens, but use plants that are spaced further apart and are arranged in a design, similar to the design of an outdoor garden space. Miniature gardens are intended to look more natural, while fairy gardens are adorned with whimsical figurines and ornaments. Usually several different types of top dressings are used together in the garden to create little paths, walkways, creek beds, or patio areas. These miniature gardens and fairy gardens are very popular with homeowners. In commercial settings, be sure the design is customized, sophisticated, and appropriate to the setting.

Miniature gardens and fairy gardens often include pathways and "water" features. They are designed to mimic an outdoor garden space.

Fairy gardens often include miniature ornamental pieces, such as bird houses, animals, stepping stones, and gardening tools.

The idea behind these gardens is to create a small, inviting, intimate space that draws the viewer into a different, imaginative world. Use plants that mimic the outdoors, including trees, flowers, shrubs, flowers, vines, and mosses, although not necessarily all in the same garden (see Table 9 for suggestions). At the very least a miniature garden or fairy garden should contain a treelike plant, some mid-sized shrublike plants, and moss or other top dressing. Mosses may be live or preserved, and add much to the gardenlike theme.

Containers should be low and made from a natural-looking material. Terra cotta pots, wooden planters, stone pots, weathered metal pots, and matte-finish fiberglass pots are used most often.

When used indoors, the decorative pots must be completely waterproof to protect the furniture on which they sit.

In these miniature gardens, the plants are taken out of their grow pots and directly planted, adding additional soil between the root balls as needed. Usually smaller plants, from plug-size to 4-inch grow pots, are used.

The tallest plant in a miniature garden should be treelike and placed slightly off-centered. Smaller, shrublike plants are then placed artistically around the central plant, with mosses and vining plants used to fill space, and planted close to the edge. Water features or small ponds can be created using a small saucer or bowl with small

stones placed around the edges for a more natural look. Finish the look with small bark nuggets as a top dressing, and pea gravel or sand to create pathways. Natural-looking elements such as interesting rocks, twigs, and woodland figurines may be added for additional interest. The larger the container, the more sophisticated and detailed the design can be.

The same design principles apply when planting fairy gardens, but the designer has more room for creativity. Fanciful figurines, miniature houses, and other decorative elements can be used. A fairy garden can be compared to a doll house, while a miniature garden is more like a designer's model home. Fairy gardens can be used commercially in children's hospitals, boutiques and other settings where the theme is quirky, imagination, or children.

Table 9. Plants for dish, miniature, and fairy gardens.

Habit	Common name	Botanical name	Notes
Treelike plants*	Arboricola	*Schefflera arboricola*	Single-stemmed tree with lower leaves removed
	Marginata	*Dracaena cincta*	—
	Ming aralia	*Polyscias fruticosa*	—
	Neanthe bella palm	*Chamaedorea elegans*	—
Shrublike plants	African violet	*Saintpaulia* hybrids	—
	Arboricola	*Schefflera arboricola*	Multistemmed bush
	Ming aralia	*Polyscias fruticosa*	—
	Succulents	*Agave* and others	—
Vining plants	Creeping fig	*Ficus pumila*	—
	English ivy	*Hedera helix*	Any miniature variety
	Heart-leaf philodendron	*Philodendron cordatum*	—
	Pothos	*Epipremnum aureum*	—
Flowering plants	African violet	*Saintpaulia* hybrids	Miniature sizes
	Azalea	*Rhododendron* hybrids	Small forms
	Begonias	*Begonia* hybrids	Small forms
	Orchids	various genera	Miniature forms
	Rose	*Rosa* varieties	Miniature varieties only; short lifespan if used indoors

*Includes taller single-stemmed plants in seedling, 2- and 4-inch sizes trimmed to resemble small trees

Terrariums

Terrariums are miniature gardens planted in clear glass or acrylic containers with walls. The containers may be closed with a top piece of glass or acrylic, be partially enclosed, or be open at the top. Terrarium planters come in all shapes and sizes, from small globes that can be hung from branches to large aquarium fish tanks, minus the water and fish. As with other types of tabletop gardens, terrariums must be completely waterproof to protect the furniture and other finishes on which they are set.

Terrariums can be used on tabletops, receptionist desks, and other areas. They can also be used in the place of a fish tank on a display table or in a niche. Larger terrariums can be used in shopping mall corridors and other public places.

For deeper terrariums, a small amount of charcoal chips (such as used in fish tank filters) mixed in with the soil medium may be added to help filter out impurities and keep the soil smelling sweet. Moss, pebbles, and other types of top dressing may be used, or the soil substrate may be kept uncovered. Terrariums are almost always direct-planted into the container.

Because terrariums create a microclimate for plants, it is vitally important to use plants that have similar watering and lighting requirements. Many terrariums, especially those with closed or partially closed tops, use plants that prefer higher levels of moisture and humidity, since the plants themselves will be creating additional humidity as they transpire. Occasionally it may be necessary to open the top of a terrarium to allow for fresh air, and to allow the medium to dry out if it becomes too wet. The sides of the terrarium can be wiped

Terrariums may be open or closed with a lid. Small terrariums may be used on desktops and tables.

Succulent terrariums should be kept open to keep the humidity low and prevent rotting.

with a moist, soft cloth if algae becomes a problem.

Most plants listed for dish, miniature, and fairy gardens will do well in terrariums. Other plants that also do well in terrariums include ferns of all types, mosses, pitcher plants, and Venus fly-traps. Succulents are increasingly popular as terrarium plants.

Due to their more humid microclimate, terrariums are very low maintenance and can do well for months without additional watering or care, especially when succulents and cacti are grown. Be careful not to overwater a terrarium—a little water will last a long time!

Plants in terrariums may require an occasional trimming to keep their shape and size within the parameters of the terrarium walls. Plants can live for a very long time in a terrarium, but may need to be replaced if they become too large.

Decorative rocks, branches, and figurines can be added to terrariums for additional interest. A miniature landscape can be created, including pathways and ponds using small glass bowls or saucers buried into the soil substrate.

In terrariums, additional care must be given to assure that all the plants are healthy, free from diseases and any pests. A terrarium can quickly become an incubator for plant pests and diseases, wiping out an entire planting quickly. If problems occur, replace the plants in question and re-plant with fresh soil if there is any chance that the pests or diseases are soil-borne.

Green Walls and Vertical Gardens

9

Green walls and vertical gardens are the fastest-growing design trends in indoor plants. Also known as biowalls or living walls, these systems are a method of growing plants on a vertical wall or trellis rather than in a planter horizontally on a floor, ledge, or table. They can be grown indoors where they may need supplemental lighting depending on their size, location, and plant selection.

Today there are green walls to fit every space, size, and budget. They can be small plaques that fit on a wall or several stories tall. They can be portable on coasters, fixed onto a wall, or permanently integrated with the building and its HVAC system. They can be simple or very complicated feats of engineering. Larger green walls almost always need the skills of a structural engineer, while smaller ones can safely be used by home owners and office workers.

Green walls help to clean the air of pollutants and soften urban noise levels while creating an oasis of green within cities. Urban green walls may be used to grow vegetables and herbs for restaurants, urban gardening projects, and school programs.

◁ Plants have been growing on the sides of cliffs and waterfalls for thousands of years.

PATRICK BLANC: FATHER OF THE MODERN GREEN WALL

Most experts agree that the father of the modern green wall is Patrick Blanc, a botanist and designer living in France and working all over the world. Blanc first started designing green walls in the 1970s, using a system he developed that used a felt material (most likely a form of capillary matting) to grow plants hydroponically on a vertical wall. His design philosophy is to mimic the jungles and rainforests which he often visited in search of new plant species, using woody shrubs near the top and low-light plants near the bottom. He uses several hundred different species and varieties of plants in his designs, once again mimicking the plant diversity found in the wild. His designs are hand-drawn in great detail, showing the location and design pattern for each variety of plant.

Blanc's designs have gained in popularity, and today they can be found all over the globe. Many of his structures are several stories tall. Some envelop the entire exterior of buildings, or mask the concrete of bridges and other urban structures. His designs now include intricate patterns of swirls and waves, mimicking the organic shapes found in nature in a more modern, contemporary way. He still prefers to use several hundred varieties of plants in his larger designs, using larger plants at the top and understory plants at the bottom, providing space for traffic to get by. He continues to inspire horticultural designers and is a sought-after expert on green walls. His work with green walls requires a great deal of expertise, and extensive knowledge of tropical and subtropical plants.

Many green walls follow Patrick Blanc's design philosophy of mimicking the designs found in nature, such as this green wall by McCaren Designs.

IRRIGATION AND WATERING

All green walls need to be watered. Some are watered by hand, while other larger systems include an irrigation system, usually a drip system with tubes running across the top of the planting area. Some systems have several horizontal lines of irrigation tubes running across the wall at different heights to provide more even watering. The irrigation system may be turned off and on manually, or set on a timer. Most larger systems use a timer.

Indoors, a green wall must be completely waterproofed. Care must be taken to protect the walls and flooring from dripping water.

A green wall may be self-contained, as with a vertical display system. Water that has drained through the system is collected in a basin at the bottom, filtered, and pumped back to the top to be re-used for irrigation. This is called a closed green wall system and must have a drainage pan underneath, with adequate width and depth to capture the drainage water.

An open green wall system also utilizes a drainage basin for excess irrigation water. Water is collected in the basin, and then drained away through the building's drainage system. Fresh water is brought in for irrigation and is not reused.

Some systems do not use a drainage pan. Instead, each plant pocket or tray is waterproofed. Excess water collects in the pocket or tray, and the plants usually take up the excess water through a subirrigation or capillary mat system. Many smaller green walls and portable walls use this type of system.

 Many green walls include a drainage pan, which is usually concealed by framing material.

TYPES OF GREEN WALLS

Green walls are best categorized according to their structure. Green Plants for Green Buildings has identified several types including vertical displays, planting pockets, engineered modular systems, fixed and modular hydroponic walls, and biofiltration walls. Each system has its benefits and challenges. Selection depends on budget, size, permanence, portability, and how and where the system will be used.

Vertical Displays

Vertical displays utilize fully grown plants in their grow pots to provide an immediately finished and visually striking green wall. Most vertical displays consist of slanted planter boxes affixed onto a grid, so the grow pots are hidden and the tops of the plants slant outward towards the viewer. The display itself may be attached to a wall, or it may be freestanding and portable.

Vertical displays are often used for special occasions and seasonal displays due to their portability and the ease of changing out plants. They are also employed in buildings where damage to the walls must be prevented. This includes historical buildings and older buildings where the walls are not structurally sound enough to support any other type of green wall system.

The planter boxes in these displays are waterproofed, making them ideal for indoor settings. Plants in 6-inch grow pots are preferred, but any size and type of plant can be used since plants remain in their grow pots. Plants should be chosen based on the amount of light available, keeping in mind that plants near the bottom will receive less light than those at the top.

A built-in watering system may be incorporated into the display, usually a drip irrigation system. Individual watering drip tubes may feed into each pot, so plants with different watering needs may be used. Another alternative is to have a feeder tube at the top of each planter box so water drips directly into the bottom of each box. In this method, capillary matting or a long capillary stake is inserted into the bottom of each plant to create a subirrigation system. All the plants in each planter box should have similar watering needs.

Individual plants may also be hand-watered. Each pot is tilted to a vertical position or removed for watering, then replaced into the planter box. This is much more labor-intensive and is rarely used except for very small vertical displays.

Pests and diseases are usually not an issue, since infected plants can easily be removed and replaced. Plants can be trimmed to maintain the design integrity.

Contemporary wall sconces can be used individually or together to create a green wall. Each sconce is watered individually, and plant size is limited to 4-inch grow pots or smaller for this particular model.

As long as the environmental conditions are right for it, any kind of plant can be grown in a vertical display. Blooming plants are a favorite since they are easily replaced when their flowers start to fade. Vertical displays are especially impactful when used in holiday displays. Designs such as a company's logo can be incorporated into the display by plotting the design on grid paper and using plants with different colors of foliage or flowers.

Vertical displays are easy to install and maintain and are relatively inexpensive. Costs vary depending on the system, type of watering system, size, and plants used. Each brand and model of green wall is different, and most manufacturers provide design and installation support for the systems they produce.

Planting Pockets and Wall Sconces

Planting pockets differ from vertical displays in several ways. First, the plants are taken out of their grow pots and planted directly into individual pockets, which may be sewn or glued onto a mat or fiberglass background. Second, planting pocket size is variable. Some pockets, such as a wall sconce, hold a single plant, while others are row-long, with room for several plants. The pockets are typically manufactured from some sort of fiber and are soft-shelled, but others are formed into hard shells made of fiberglass. Most hard-shelled pockets are known as wall sconces.

Wall sconces in fiberglass and plastic are setting new trends in design and becoming very

These moss-lined wall sconces partially cover an ugly concrete wall and add a touch of tropical elegance to this interior space in Hawaii.

popular, especially in homes, offices, and smaller indoor spaces. They are often available as modules in several different sizes. The modules can be fitted together, like pieces of a jigsaw puzzle, to create interesting wall designs. Wall sconce pockets can be used for holding other objects such as notepads and books, mixed with pockets of plants. This makes an attractive and functional addition to homes and small offices, while taking advantage of the many benefits that live plants offer.

Planting pockets may be used indoors or outdoors, depending on their design and material. Fiber pockets may not be waterproofed, while most hard-shelled pockets are waterproof. Some hard-shelled pockets are made to fit onto a wall grid and can be re-arranged to suit the changing needs of the owners.

Pocket systems that are not waterproofed are normally restricted to outdoor locations, since drainage from the pockets, both at the bottom and the sides, is likely to damage the walls, floors, and whatever else is adjacent to the systems.

When planting pocket green wall systems, additional substrate may be needed to raise the soil ball up to 1 or 2 inches below the rim of the pocket, and to fill in the sides. Usually no top dressing is needed, since the plants are nearly upright and foliage hides the top of the substrate from view. Seldom is drainage material needed, unless the pocket is significantly deeper than the root ball. The soil medium usually does not wash out unless the pockets are watered too forcibly or the plants are overwatered. Most pocket systems are hand-watered and do not include an irrigation system. Drip irrigation is used on larger pocket systems.

Fibrous pockets are very popular for planting herbs, vegetables, and flowers along outdoor walls and fences. Fiber pocket systems are relatively inexpensive and are used by many home owners.

Engineered Modular Systems

Engineered modular systems are composed of building blocks of green wall systems, pre-planted and placed together on a grid that is attached to the wall of the building. Modular systems are frequently used for large installations in atriums, lobbies, and outdoor spaces. Most include an irrigation system, which can be placed on a timer, and a drainage system, which may or may not recirculate the drainage water. Most modular systems require a growing-in period of three to six months or more prior to installation, so the plants can reach a size where they can make a visual impact.

Each module is composed of a square-shaped box made out of metal or heavy plastic, with a metal grid or molded pockets on the front face for planting. The modules are filled with a soilless medium into which cuttings or seedlings are planted at the greenhouse or nursery. The modules are laid horizontally on tables and grown to a designated size for three to six months before the finished product is ready for shipping.

Preserved moss may be attached to the surface, surrounding each plant, to help retain the soilless medium before shipping the modules to the horticultural contractor or directly to the site. If there is a delay in installation, the modules are best held at a greenhouse or nursery where the plants can continue to grow.

Before bolting the metal grid platform to the wall of the building, a waterproof barrier is attached to make sure no structural damage is caused by any leaks in the system. This requires the professional services of a structural engineer to make sure the wall can support the green wall system, especially once it is wet.

If a drip irrigation system is wanted, it should be installed on the grid before or during the installation of the modules. Feeder tubes are placed horizontally at different heights to make sure watering is as uniform as possible. The system should be tested to make sure there are no "dry" spots on the wall.

A drainage pan is placed at the bottom of the system to catch the water as it drips down the green wall and through the modules. This water will contain minerals and salts leached from the soilless medium. In an open system, the drainage pan is plumbed so the water exits through the building's plumbing system. In a closed system, a filter and pump are installed to remove excess minerals from the drainage water before recirculating the water back through the green wall.

Modular systems should be kept moist at all times to prevent the development of dry pockets in the medium. Water will tend to run off and around any dry pockets within the medium without giving the plants the water they need.

Care must be taken that all plants are free from pests and diseases, since any infestations will spread quickly throughout the wall. Most problems can be kept under control by regularly cleaning and trimming the plants, as well as proper watering. Systemic fungicides and pesticides, along with fertilizer solution, can be added to the watering system to keep the green wall healthy if these preventative measures are not adequate. Applying systemics through the watering system limits the exposure of both the horticulturist and general public, since the chemicals

are contained within the system and are not airborne. Any spray applications of pesticides should be done during off hours to minimize exposure to the public, using the safest controls available.

Since most modular systems are large, they require regular maintenance by professionals, both for the plants and for the mechanics of the system itself. This maintenance should be built into the building's budget to maintain the value and protect the investment in a large green wall, and keep it looking its best.

Modular systems tend to weigh more due to their size, the materials used for the planting boxes, and the weight of keeping the soil medium moist at all times. They also tend to be more costly due to their size; the need for pre-planting and growing plants to size at the greenhouse or nursery; shipping the pre-planted modules; materials used for the systems and wall grid; the requirement of a building engineer and other building professionals; and the labor involved in growing, delivering, and installing the system. They are one of the best choices for larger green wall installations and, with proper care, can last for decades.

Hydroponic Walls

Hydroponic walls contain no soil or organic substrate. Plants are grown in a fibrous material such as rock wool or a type of capillary matting, where water runs freely through the material. The plants must be grown from seedlings or rooted cuttings that themselves have been grown hydroponically in a similar medium. Due to the high level of evaporation, most hydroponic walls are

Large modular systems require the collaboration of building engineers and horticulturists for a safe installation.

This large modular green wall is maintained by the trained professional horticulturists at Longwood Gardens. It is one of the largest green walls in North America.

Hydroponic walls utilize bare-root plant cuttings and contain no soil medium.

used indoors. A structural engineer is required to assist with planning and installing larger hydroponic walls.

Smaller hydroponic walls can be manufactured as a single unit, which is hung on a grid structure on the wall. Many larger hydroponic systems are modular, with blocks of units that are hung individually on the grid structure, similar to an engineered modular system. All hydroponic systems require a drip irrigation system, which can be placed on a timer.

Proper fertilization with a complete fertilizer containing all of the macronutrients and micronutrients that plants need to survive is critically important, since the hydroponic medium contains no nutrients. A drainage pan is required, and excess water may be filtered and recirculated through the system, or evacuated through the building's plumbing system.

Plants on a hydroponic system grow a vigorous root system and tend to have fewer soil-borne diseases or pests since there is no organic matter in the growing medium. Over time, the roots become interwoven into the medium, which may make replacing individual plants much more difficult. The system must be checked regularly to ensure that no dry pockets have developed, although this is much less likely to occur with a hydroponic system.

Bare-root plugs or cuttings are planted in the system, usually at the greenhouse or nursery, and grown to an established size prior to shipping the system to the building's site. Hydroponic systems tend to be higher priced due to the cost of the materials, growing time in the nursery, shipping costs, and the need for building professionals such as a structural engineer. Regular maintenance of both the plants and the mechanics of the system are required.

Biofiltration Walls

Biofiltration walls, or biowalls, are a highly specialized green wall system that is integrated with the building's HVAC system and becomes a permanent fixture of the building. Most biowalls are hydroponic systems. They are attached to a support grid, which in turn is attached to the building's wall. A structural engineer and mechanical engineer are required during the installation process. Since they are part of the HVAC system, all biowalls are indoor green wall systems and these are not used outdoors.

In a biowall, a building's air is pulled through the plants and their hydroponic medium into the HVAC system. As with other indoor plants, the microbes growing in the medium convert volatile organic compounds into harmless compounds that the plants then utilize for food. Moisture is also added to the air, increasing humidity levels to more comfortable levels. This clean air is then recirculated throughout the building by the HVAC system. The ability of indoor plants to clean the air is greatly enhanced with this system.

Biowalls require the same care as other green wall systems. Most biowalls are large, often several stories high, and a lift system is usually required for their maintenance. The costs of a biowall are high and the system is patented by NedLaw Living Walls, the only company currently selling this system. NedLaw usually performs the installation to insure its successful integration into the building's HVAC system.

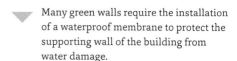

Many green walls require the installation of a waterproof membrane to protect the supporting wall of the building from water damage.

A drainage pan and a waterproofed support wall are required as with engineered modular systems. Care must be taken to ensure the health of the plants, including regular inspections and treatment for any pests or diseases. Biowalls require a complete fertilizer to provide the plants with all of their nutritional needs. Biowalls can last for many years if they are properly maintained.

PROFESSIONAL INSTALLATION AND MAINTENANCE

Smaller green walls, especially those that are freestanding, require no structural building support and therefore no assistance from an engineer for their safe installation. Larger freestanding green walls may require an engineer's help to make sure the floor has enough weight-bearing capacity to support a wet, planted green wall and possibly the irrigation system. In contrast, green walls that are mounted on a wall, especially an indoor wall, usually require building engineers and other professionals to assist in their planning and installation. According to Green Plants for Green Buildings, some of the issues to be considered by these experts include the following:

- The weight-bearing capacity of the building's wall and floor.
- A waterproofing barrier on the building's wall for protection.
- A way to capture and remove drainage water.
- Installation of the supporting grid system.
- Installation of supplemental lighting as needed.
- Installation of a lift system for maintaining taller walls, and its storage.
- Installation of an irrigation system as needed.

In addition to installation professionals, most green walls require the recommendations and care of a professional horticulturist who can plan for the overall health and longevity of the plants. This individual can help with the following tasks:

- Plant selection, dependent primarily on the lighting available.
- Assistance with supplemental lighting.
- Selection and installation of an irrigation system.
- Design of the planting itself.
- Overseeing the growing of any pre-planted modules, their safe delivery, storage, and installation.
- Developing and carrying out a maintenance program for the wall and its plantings.

Since the plants on a green wall are grown vertically, supplemental lighting for larger systems is usually required. The bottom portion of a green wall will receive much lower light levels than the top. A professional horticulturist will take light measure readings at various levels on a green wall, at various times of the day, to determine how much supplemental lighting may be needed, and which plants will grow the best in different portions of the green wall. Directional spot lights are usually used to provide the supplemental lighting required.

DESIGNING A GREEN WALL

A green wall is very much like a living painting, a piece of art that changes over time. Designs can be formal or informal, complex or very simple. More formal arrangements will require more maintenance, trimming, and pruning to maintain the design.

Supplemental lighting is often required to keep a green wall healthy and looking good, especially for plants located on the lower section of the wall.

A schematic drawing gives the site's owner an excellent idea of what the green wall will look like, and acts as a guide for the installation and planting.

When designing a green wall, begin by drawing the basic design concept on paper in scale to the dimensions of the green wall. Designate the colors for each form within the design. Then plot out the placement of each plant, according to the color and size of its pot.

If you are using a modular system, you must also plot out each module in the design. Number each module, particularly on larger green walls, so the modules can be placed in the correct position once they are assembled. This process is much like creating a jigsaw puzzle, manufacturing, and numbering each piece, and then putting the jigsaw puzzle together.

Keep in mind that the green wall will be hanging vertically, and that plants may droop downward according to their species. Ferns, vining plants, and plants with long, strappy leaves will droop down. Succulents and mosses will tend to stay more compact with less drooping. A mix of forms will add interest to the green wall.

Use plants with various colors of foliage from dark burgundies to neon green to add more impact and pattern to the design. Plants with variegated, multicolored leaves such as crotons will also add interest.

Shorter plants will tend to curve upward towards the light. This may result in some plants that are J-shaped drooping down in the middle with the tips bending upwards. All this must be considered when designing a green wall.

Plants with different colors and textures bring out the design and make a green wall more interesting. This project by LiveWall won an award in an art competition.

If blooming plants will be included in the green wall, keep in mind that they will only be in flower for a few weeks. Use blooming plants that also have foliage that will fit into your design, or use a system that allows for quick and easy replacement of blooming plants. Here are some clever ways a green wall can be used to enhance the design of a space:

- Diagonal lines of various colors, perhaps with blooming plants running across the center.

- Concentric squares or rectangles forming frames within frames of various colors, perhaps with blooming plants placed in the center.

- A company's logo replicated using plants of different colors.

- An aerial photograph of the area, reproduced in plants.

- A local landmark re-created in plants.

- Swirls of plants in different colors, using organic shapes.

- A mixture of plants placed in clumps to mimic nature.

- Re-creation of a well-known piece of art, designed in plants of appropriate colors.

The more natural the design, the less maintenance will be required. A natural look is easy to maintain, while more formalized patterns will require regular trimming and care to keep the design intact.

A green wall fits nicely into an oddly shaped niche in a very contemporary home in Australia.

Green walls flank the company's logo for business known for its creativity and innovation.

Green walls can also be used for seasonal displays. After the holidays, the poinsettias are replaced with foliage plants.

Green walls can brighten up an otherwise dark space, such as this retail display area.

These stately palms in the World Financial Center Winter Gardens are watered individually with a fully automated 16-zone irrigation system.

Watering Indoor Plants

Interior plantscapes always look so beautiful when they are first installed. The plants are pristine, the top dressing impeccable, and everything fits perfectly together. After a few weeks, reality sets in. The plants are shedding their leaves and growing awkwardly, searching for light. Some have developed spots or brown edges and tips on their once-flawless leaves. The top dressing is messed up and missing in spots. Everything looks dusty and you see some gnats flying around that weren't there before. In other words, the magic is gone.

Professional horticulturists know how to "keep the magic" in a design for many years to come. Plants are living, breathing, growing organisms that need water, light, and regular care. Tricks of the trade can be used to maintain the original design intent and keep the interiorscape beautiful, healthy, and up-to-date.

When designing an interior plantscape, mechanisms to aid in the care of the planting must be taken into consideration. These may include hose bibs and stepping stones in gardens, and lifts for tall green walls. Plants on tall ledges may require eye hooks in the walls to which safety ropes and harnesses can be attached. Above all, the safety of the people taking care of the plants, as well as the general public, must always be a top priority in any design.

Providing adequate lighting and choosing plants according to the light available have been discussed in previous chapters and are critically important to the health and longevity of indoor plants. Without adequate lighting, no amount of care will ensure healthy plants and they will soon begin to deteriorate, creating an uphill battle for horticulturist and owner alike.

THE HORTICULTURE TECHNICIAN

The person who takes care of indoor plants for a living is usually called a horticulture technician, or tech. You may also hear that individual referred to as a horticultural engineer, horticulturist, account manager, or simply the plant lady or man. The job of a horticultural technician is challenging, physically demanding, and very rewarding. Most of the people who do it are good at problem-solving and they love to learn more about plants. They tend to be very nurturing towards people and plants alike.

A college degree is not required to become a horticultural technician. Most horticultural technicians are trained on the job, under a senior technician or supervisor for several weeks, and then receive additional training from their employer throughout the year. A few colleges and universities offer a single course in interior plantscaping as part of their two- or four-year horticulture degree program. In addition, further training and education are available at conferences and through private training companies such as Johnson Fediw Associates (owned by the author).

The National Association of Landscape Professionals offers certification for interior plantscape technicians through the Landscape Industry Certified Interior Technician (formerly CLT-I) program. This intermediate-to-advanced self-study program requires a score of 70 percent to pass the exam. Certification is not required to work in this field, but it certainly sets those who have it apart from other job applicants. Most certified technicians can expect to earn a higher pay rate, and they are more likely to be considered for promotion.

WHY WATER IS ESSENTIAL FOR PLANTS

After light, the second most important factor in the longevity of indoor plants is proper watering. Plants need water for a number of purposes. The majority of a plant's tissues are composed of water. Water (as well as other materials) is the primary component of the center of a plant's cells, where it presses against the semi-rigid sides of the cells and makes a plant crisp and sturdy. This pressure is called turgor pressure and allows plants to stand upright. Thinner cell walls make a plant more delicate and prone to wilting when it does not get enough water. Most plants that wilt easily, such as peace lilies (*Spathiphyllum*) and chrysanthemums, have thinner cell walls. The thinner the walls, the more delicate the plant.

Water is also an important component in most metabolic processes within a plant. Photosynthesis, for example, requires water for the chemical process to take place. Respiration, or the conversion of stored carbohydrates into energy, also requires water. So water plays an important role in the creation of new stems, leaves, flowers, and seeds, and in the overall growth of a plant. Plants that do not have adequate water over a period of time tend to lose their coloring and stop growing. In fact, they will lose their leaves because there isn't enough water to maintain the cells, and so they die. The net result is that the plant conserves water by losing its leaves, an adaption that allows plants to survive in some very harsh conditions.

Water transports nutrients from the soil into a plant's roots through osmosis. Nutrients and minerals are dissolved in the soil medium, transported across the cell membranes in roots and root hairs, and then pulled up the plant's stem or trunk to the leaves, buds, lateral stems, and flowers.

Despite the importance of the role that water plays in a plant, only a small amount of water that a plant takes up from the soil is used within

a plant's cells and for metabolic processes. The majority of water that a plant takes up is lost and released back into the atmosphere through transpiration, which discharges water in the form of vapor through the stomates, or pores, on the

Watering plants takes up the majority of a horticulture technician's time when taking care of indoor plants.

Greenhouses and conservatories tend to be very humid, due in part to the large number of plants transpiring water vapor into the air.

leaves. This process occurs continuously through-out the day, slowing down in darkness. Plants in lower light levels have a slower rate of transpiration, and they take up water from the soil more slowly, so they don't need to be watered as often as plants in high light.

Transpiration helps to keep a plant cool as vapor disperses, but if conditions get too hot, or if a plant has dried out, the stomates on the leaves tend to close, shutting down the process and drastically slowing the uptake of water. Frequently the leaves will curl, minimizing the exposure of stomates to open air and reducing the rate of transpiration. In effect, the plant decreases the water lost through transpiration so it can conserve water within its cells and use what it has for survival.

Transpiration creates a vacuum within the xylem, the tubes through which water and dis-solved nutrients are transported into various parts of a plant. This vacuum pulls water up into the plant from the soil and roots, all the way to the very top. Without transpiration, a plant would only be able to pull water up into its leaves and buds a short distance. There would be no majestic 60- to 100-foot trees, and our environment would be far less interesting.

Another benefit of transpiration is that it increases the humidity in a room. In a greenhouse, this increase is quite evident due to the large number of plants. In an office space with one or two plants, the increase in humidity is not as noticeable, but transpiration still helps to raise the humidity to levels that are more comfortable.

HOW WATER MOVES THROUGH SOIL

In moist soil, a thin layer of water molecules surrounds each particle of soil, along with the nutrients it carries. As a root pulls the water away from the soil particles it touches, water is pulled slowly and steadily through the soil medium to replace it. If the soil medium dries out too much, the layers of water molecules no longer exist and water ceases to move through the soil. Instead of penetrating through the root ball, water will tend to run off the medium. In this situation, a liquid wetting agent can be added to the water to help the water penetrate through the root ball, re-wet the soil, and re-create the layers of water molecules on each particle. Several wetting agents are available through greenhouse suppliers, or some liquid soap can be used if no other wetting agents are available.

When using liquid soap as a wetting agent, a little goes a long way. Two or three drops in a gallon of water are all you need. Any mild liquid soap will work, such as Ivory liquid or Murphy oil soap. Anti-bacterial soaps (which will not control plant diseases) and grease-cutting dish detergents have been known to damage plants in hot, sunny areas and should not be used. A treatment once every six to eight weeks or longer is usually sufficient to keep any watering problems under control.

Do not use liquid soap or any wetting agents with plants in subirrigation systems. This will cause them to stay too wet for long periods of time, leading to root rot. Using too much soap may result in a build-up of phosphates or burning of the roots, and should be avoided.

BASIC RULES FOR WATERING PLANTS

Most plants prefer to be a little too dry than to be too wet, so if in doubt it is usually best to wait before watering a plant again. When making a decision on whether or not to water a plant that is in between being wet or being dry, consider the environment, type of plant, type of medium, and your own schedule.

If the plant is in a sunny, hot, dry environment, a little water will help to tide it over until your next visit. If the environment is cool or in low light, the plant can usually last another week or two before watering again without any ill effects.

Certain plants use water more rapidly than others that are more capable of storing water in their tissues and should be watered if there is any question about their status. These plants include peace lily (*Spathiphyllum*), weeping fig tree (*Ficus benjamina*), fiddleleaf fig (*Ficus lyrata*), areca palm (*Dypsis* lutescens), pygmy date palm (*Phoenix roebelenii*), and many flowering plants, especially azaleas, chrysanthemums, cyclamens, and poinsettias.

The plant maintenance schedule also plays a role in deciding whether or not it is time to water. If the horticulturist is returning within a week, the plant can usually wait. If the horticulturist will not be able to check plant for two weeks or longer, water the plant.

A few simple rules for watering indoor plants always apply, no matter what variety of plant, size, location, or soil medium. Once a plant is properly watered, its overall care becomes much, much easier. A plant that is properly watered will have very few problems with leaves yellowing and dropping or with leaf tips turning brown or edges that require trimming. Furthermore, the plant itself will have very few disease problems, especially root rot or leaf spot disease. Instead, the plant will exhibit strong, healthy, consistent growth, and it will be more likely to fight off and recuperate quickly from any pest problems, especially fungus gnats.

So, the three rules to follow when watering plants are

1. Always check the soil medium first to see if the plant needs water.

2. Water all around the pot's surface with lukewarm water until a little drains out of the bottom of the grow pot.

3. Dump out any excess water—don't allow a plant to sit in water for more than two hours.

That's it! It's that simple, and that complicated.

Rule #1: Check the Soil Medium

Before watering any plant, whether it's a cactus or a fern, always check the soil medium to see if it's moist or dry. Check to the depth of where the root ball begins. This may be at the surface, halfway down, near the bottom or in between, depending on the maturity and type of plant.

One way to determine the location of the top of the root ball is by sticking your finger into the soil medium. The top of the root ball will feel solid and your finger will not penetrate further without exerting pressure. If the soil medium feels moist, the plant does not need to be watered. If the soil medium feels dry, it's time to water the plant.

Sometimes it is not safe to stick your finger into the soil medium, especially if the plant has recently been treated with chemicals or if it is located in a public area. The public tends to treat indoor plants as if they are garbage cans, frequently depositing in plant pots hypodermic needles, chicken bones, cigarette butts, and things that are too disgusting to mention.

A safer way to test the soil is with a soil probe—a metal or plastic rod with a pointed end and notches cut into the sides in regularly measured intervals. Press the probe into the pot until you hit resistance and notice how far this is on the soil probe. Continue pressing until you reach the bottom (or close to the bottom) of the pot. Then give the probe a quarter turn and remove it. Feel the soil medium in each notch to see how far down the soil has dried. Note that a dry medium tends to fall out of the notch as a dry powder, while a moist medium remains in clumps. If the medium is dry down to the top of the root ball, it is time to water. If the medium is moist, do not water and check again in a week or two.

Whether using your finger or a soil probe, be sure to check in two or three locations in the grow pot. One side of the pot may be dry, while the other side may be moist, particularly if the plant does not have a healthy root system or if it is not being watered properly. If only one side is dry, water only that side of the pot.

Using a soil probe is not only safer and healthier for the person checking the plant, it is also better for the plant. The probe helps to keep the medium loose and aerated, increasing the fresh oxygen in the soil. If the medium has been overwatered, loosening it can help it dry out faster. Soil probes can also be used to poke holes in the soil, making it easier to re-wet a plant's root ball if

 Soil probes, such as this model, are a great tool for checking for soil moisture levels safely and easily.

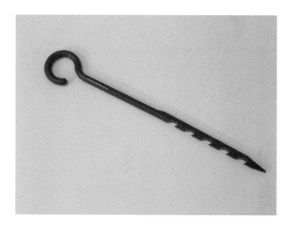

the medium has become too dry and water is rolling off the top without penetrating to the roots. Using a soil probe does not harm roots—any root pruning that occurs is minimal and does not harm the plant.

Soil probes should be disinfected on a regular basis, usually using rubbing alcohol. Soil-borne pests and diseases can be spread from one plant to another by using the same soil probe. To disinfect a probe, wipe it off with an alcohol wipe or dip it into a bottle of rubbing alcohol. Hydrogen peroxide or bleach should not be used indoors, since any spills can remove the dyes from furniture or carpets.

If the smell of alcohol bothers you—many people don't like the smell because it reminds them of a hospital or doctor's office—mix a little vanilla extract in with the rubbing alcohol to mask the odor. Inexpensive, artificially flavored vanilla extract works just as well as the gourmet brands at a fraction of the cost. Other flavors can also be used, but vanilla is universally liked by most people. Vanilla extract also works well to mask any odors if you need to apply a pesticide.

Avoid spraying rubbing alcohol when indoors. Rubbing alcohol is very irritating to the eyes, nose and throat, especially for those with respiratory problems.

Rule #2:
Water All Around the Pot with Lukewarm Water

When a plant is top-watered (water is added to the top of the soil) it is important to water all the way around the pot, not on one side alone. Water

moves primarily vertically downward in soil, not horizontally. For example, when watering the lawn, no one stands in one corner with a hose and hopes the water gets to the other side. Instead, the entire surface of the lawn is watered. The same principle is applied when watering indoor plants, whether they are in individual pots or directly planted in a garden.

Watering on one side only may result in dry spots that then become difficult to re-wet. Roots may die in the dry areas, and the damage shows up as dead stems, branches, and foliage on that side of the plant.

The water used should be lukewarm at about the same temperature as you would use to bathe a baby. Remember that most indoor plants are tropical or subtropical plants and respond well to warm water. If the water is too cold, the roots suffer chill damage and that damage spreads up into the leaves, discoloring and damaging them. If the water is too hot, the roots boil and become damaged with the results showing on the foliage as well.

Lukewarm water should be between 65 and 78 degrees Fahrenheit, but there is no need to be exact. As long as the water is comfortable to the touch and close to room temperature, the plants will do fine. Over time, this makes a difference in the overall health and appearance of indoor plants.

In some buildings, only cold water is available for watering plants. If this is the case, keep in mind that the plants will most likely suffer from damage, especially when the temperatures outside are cold, too. Choose plants that are more tolerant to cold temperatures, and avoid plants such as older varieties of aglaonemas that are very sensitive to cold.

Rule #3: Dump Out Any Excess Water

When watering plants in their grow pots, give the plant enough water that a little excess runs through the grow pot and into the saucer or drainage portion of the decorative container. Listen for the sound of water dripping through, or pull away some of the top dressing to see what is going on.

This type of watering is called leaching and serves two purposes. First, leaching removes excess soluble salts and minerals (mostly from fertilizer) that can build up and damage a plant. Secondly, leaching washes away stale air from the pores of the medium and pulls fresh oxygen into the soil. Roots need oxygen to survive and grow.

Plants will usually take up any excess drainage water that they are exposed to within 24 hours, most of that within the first two hours. For plants that were too dry, this can ensure that the soil medium is wet throughout, but if plants are allowed to sit in standing water for an extended period, problems such as root rot can occur.

To see if excess water is accumulating in the bottom of the pot, use a long dip stick down the side of the decorative container to the bottom, then pull it back up to see the water level. A strawlike tube of Plexiglas can also be used by putting your thumb over the top, creating a vacuum, and checking the level of water in the tube. Another method is to pull away some of the top dressing and staging materials from one area of the decorative container and use a flash light to peek inside.

Plants do not like to sit in water for more than a couple of hours. When a plant is sitting in water, the pores in the soil medium fill with water instead of oxygen, which the roots need to breathe and function properly. Roots will literally drown and die if they remain sitting in excess water for long periods. This is the primary reason for elevating plants slightly above the saucer or bottom of the pot, so they are not actually sitting in excess drainage water.

The excess water, along with the soluble salts that have leached out, can be taken back up again into the soil if it is not drained out. They will eventually build up in the soil and cause soluble salts damage, which appears as burned tips and edges on the foliage and root damage. In time, the excess drainage water can accumulate if it is not pumped or drained out. Roots and the organic matter in the soil medium will start to rot, creating a smelly mess that will greatly disturb the occupants and visitors to the building.

Excess water can be removed by taking containers outdoors and dumping out the surplus water. Turkey basters can also be used if the amount of water is small. If the containers cannot be removed, a portable pump may be needed.

SUBIRRIGATION SYSTEMS

Subirrigation systems help plants grow better by watering them from the bottom rather than the top. Most such systems work by the process of capillary action. Water is held in a reservoir beneath the plant and released slowly into the soil medium. As the water moves vertically upward throughout the medium (instead of vertically downward as with top-watering methods), the plant's roots pull it out of the soil, just as with top-watering.

Because plants are elevated above the reservoir, they are therefore never actually sitting in water. Hydroponic systems, however, work a little differently and will be discussed later. Subirrigation systems evenly moisten the entire root ball throughout, with no dry pockets of soil medium. The horticulturist must still check the soil for moisture and wait until the top of the root ball feels dry to the touch before adding more water to the reservoir.

The reservoir usually holds a larger quantity of water in storage for a plant's upcoming needs, than if the plant was top-watered. Therefore, plants on subirrigation systems do not require watering as often, saving the horticulturist from needing to care for the plant as often as a top-watered plant. This saves time and money and can improve the profitability of the plant care company. The client, their guests, and employees are not interrupted as often by frequent horticultural visits. Fewer visits mean less carbon emissions from vehicles used to visit the site, so everyone wins with subirrigation.

The systems are overall more environmentally friendly than top-watering. Plants are healthier and less likely to develop diseases that may require care or replacement. Any pesticides and fertilizers applied to the soil can be diluted, cutting the dosage by half, since none is leached out and wasted. Any excess soluble salts and minerals are rinsed upwards and collect on top surface of the soil medium where they can be scraped off and easily removed.

Subirrigation also provides even and consistent watering, no matter which horticulturist is caring for the plants. Each horticulture technician tends to develop their own personal style of caring for plants, even if they are trained by the same person. When a new technician takes over the care, for whatever reason, plants tend to react to this change, even if it is only for one plant care visit. Plants adapt to the watering style of their regular horticulturist, and when someone else waters them slightly differently, they tend to lose a few leaves due to the change. The other horticulturist is probably doing a good job caring for the plants—their methods are just slightly different. It's as if the plants "miss" their regular caregiver and throw a temper tantrum in response. With subirrigation, the watering is always the same.

When designing the interiorscape, take into consideration what type of subirrigation system you may need to maintain the health and longevity of the plants. Some systems are made for certain types of decorative containers, while others need to be installed prior to planting.

Subirrigation systems can be categorized according to how they function. Those categories include fiber wick systems, soil wick systems, vacuum sensor systems, and hydroponics. All work well, although their installation and costs vary.

Fiber Wick Systems

Fiber wick subirrigation systems are fairly easy to use and inexpensive. Plants remain in their grow pots and are elevated in a waterproof container. Container plants and some vertical display green walls utilize fiber wick systems.

The fiber wick is a strip of capillary matting, a porous material similar to quilt batting, which can be cut into circles or strips. Capillary matting lasts for several years, until minerals or algae build up and make the matting less absorbent. Plants are usually elevated above the bottom of the water-proof container by 1 to 3 inches or more, creating a water reservoir beneath. The device used to elevate the plant is called a riser and can be made of various materials. Manufactured risers are usually grid-shaped and made from plastic. Home-made risers include rings of 4-to 6-in.-diameter PVC piping cut into donutlike rings at the home improvement store or with a hack saw; blocks of styrene or Styrofoam; brick or stone or similar material. Cardboard should never be used as a riser since it will collapse and rot once wet.

A strip of fiber is pushed through a drainage hole in the bottom of the grow pot, using a dip stick, screw driver, scissors, or similar instrument. The strip should be pushed into the center of the root ball. If the plant prefers to stay moist, the strip should be pushed almost to the top of the grow pot, but never showing above the soil medium. Larger plants and those that need more water may have two, three, or more strips, each in a different drainage hole. Plants that prefer to dry out more in between waterings may only have one or two strips. Water is added to the bottom of the water-proof container and is absorbed by the wick and taken up into the soil media. Most of the water is absorbed into the pot within 24 to 48 hours.

Plants in 6-inch grow pots or smaller can use a capillary wick in a different way. A piece of capillary matting is cut into a circle to fit the bottom of a deep dish plant saucer or drainage tray. This circle of matting is usually referred to as a "cap mat." The grow pot with the plant is not elevated but is placed directly onto the mat and water is added to the bottom. The grow pot must have drainage holes at the bottom, not the sides, for this version of the system to work. Some of the

To install a capillary wick, push the wick through a drainage hole into the center of the root ball, using a soil probe, screwdriver, scissors, or pencil.

fiber will be in direct contact with the soil medium, so the water is able to move up the wick and into the soil. The mat absorbs the water added to the drainage saucer within an hour or two so the plant does not remain sitting in water. Plants that need more water may require two or three layers of capillary matting.

In some cases the fiber wicking will need to be moistened first to prime the system. If the reservoir runs dry, the wick may need to be moistened again to re-start the system. The plant itself may also need to be watered if the soil medium is dry.

Fiber wick systems can be manufactured versions or home-made systems using capillary matting from a greenhouse supplier and risers made from materials found at the home improvement or hobby store. Costs vary but are usually quite inexpensive compared to some of the other systems. Plants usually need to be watered half as often as they would if they were top-watered. Thus a plant that needed watering every week may only need watering once every two weeks when placed on a fiber wick subirrigation system.

Soil Wick Systems

In soil wick systems, a plug of soil acts as the wick. All soil wick systems are manufactured from plastic and are available in a variety of sizes, depending on the manufacturer. A few incorporate the decorative container, or are specifically made and marketed to fit a particular line of ornamental containers.

In a soil wick system, the plant is taken out of its grow pot and planted directly into the system, so it is labor intensive. The soil wick system is composed of a waterproof plastic pot similar in size to a grow pot, with a removable plastic platform that sits on a ridge an inch or two above the bottom of the pot. The platform contains a cone-shaped cage that dips down into the bottom area of the pot once in place. Generally the cage has a number of drainage holes. Usually there is a column on one side of the grow pot for adding water, and for a bobber to indicate the level of the water at the bottom of the pot.

The cone-shaped cage is filled with a soil medium or LECA (Lightweight Expanded Clay Aggregate) pebbles depending on the system, and the platform is placed on the ridge inside the pot. A light layer of substrate is added to the platform before the plant is taken out of its grow pot and placed on the platform. Sometimes the root ball needs a little trimming to fit into the subirrigation pot. The top of the soil medium should be an inch or so below the rim of the pot. Additional soil may be added along the sides as needed to fill any gaps, then water is added to fill the reservoir at the bottom of the pot, checking the level with the bobber or a dip stick.

Plants in soil wick systems can usually last two to three times longer between waterings than those that are top-watered. As with all plants, the soil medium should be checked first before adding more water to the reservoir. Plants will take up the water through the soil cone slowly over time. If the medium becomes too wet, any excess water will drain out and back into the reservoir through the drainage holes in the bottom of the platform. If too much water is added to the reservoir, however, the plant may become soaked as the level of water reaches above the platform and into the root ball.

A vacuum sensor subirrigation system uses a double-walled pot as the grow pot. Water is added to at the top and fills in the space between the double walls. The vacuum sensor, located at the tip of the plastic tube, is inserted into the root ball and turns the system off and on as the soil dries out and is then re-wetted.

Vacuum Sensor Systems

Vacuum sensor subirrigation systems are manufactured exclusively by Tournesol Siteworks and work differently from the wick systems. The plants are taken out of their grow pots and set directly into the system. In one model, the system may be built into the decorative container and they are one unit. In another model, the system takes the place of the grow pot. Whereas fiber wick and soil wick systems are made for indoor use only, the vacuum sensor system may also be used outdoors.

The pot in this system is double-walled, sealed, and waterproof with a water inlet disc at the bottom of the inside wall. A hole on the top rim allows water to be poured into the space between the two walls, which is the water reservoir itself. Compared to wick systems, the vacuum sensor system holds a large quantity of water, and indoor plants can last for at least a month between waterings, sometimes two to three months or more.

Once the reservoir is filled, the hole is capped off with a rubber cork which must be tightly screwed into place. A thin layer of soil medium is added to the bottom of the pot, covering the water inlet disc. The plant is taken out of its grow pot and planted into the pot with additional soil as needed to fill any gaps.

A small hollow, narrow, flexible tube is attached to the side of the inner wall, piercing the wall and sealed into place. At the other end of the tube is a rod of ceramic material which acts as the soil moisture indicator and must be moistened just before installation. Make a tunnel into the root ball with a pencil or dip stick and insert the tube and soil moisture indicator firmly into the tunnel into the center of the root ball. If the plant needs to be kept more moist, insert the tube in a slightly upward angle so the moisture indicator is near the top of the root ball. If the plant prefers to dry out more between waterings, insert the tube and

Plants in hydroponic systems are grown bare-root in LECA pebbles. Rock wool is often used instead of pebbles when growing plants for laboratory use or when growing edible plants such as tomatoes and herbs.

indicator in a slightly downward angle towards the bottom of the root ball.

To prime the system and start it working, moisten the soil medium, fill the sides of the pot with water, and screw the rubber cork tightly into place. The plant will start using water and slowly the soil medium will begin to dry out from the top downward. Once the soil dries down to the location of the moisture indicator, the sensor will release water from the sides of the pot, through the water inlet disc at the bottom, into the soil medium. This will continue until water rises in

the soil to the location of the sensor. The system will then automatically turn itself off and water will cease to flow.

As the medium dries out again, water will be released and the cycle begins again. In this system, the soil near the bottom always remains moist, and the soil at the top always remains dry. Water can be added to the reservoir at any time. The system is nearly foolproof and the plant adapts to this type of watering very quickly.

All this takes place without electricity, batteries, or any other power source. The system works on the vacuum created between the sensor and the double-walled water reservoir. It is crucially important that the rubber cork remain firmly screwed into the watering hole at the top rim, or the vacuum will be released and the system will flood. The vacuum is released for a very short period when water is added, but only a small amount of water is released and it is of no consequence.

This system is more expensive to use than most wick systems, but plants can last for a very long time between waterings and the plants do quite well with this system. The initial costs are usually returned in lower labor costs and lower plant replacement costs within a short period. When the system is used outdoors, the labor costs are even more significant.

or cuttings and be grown entirely without soil to prevent the growth of rot. Hydroponic systems today are used primarily by hobbyists, some green wall systems, and some high-value vegetable and orchid growers.

Plants grown bare-root in water adapt to this environment and develop a different type of root system that survives in water. A complete fertilizer containing all the nutrients a plant requires must be added to the water, since no nutrients are available through soil. Plants are generally quite healthy on these systems, since there are no soil-borne diseases or pests. Many plants have lived for 30 to 50 years or more on hydroponic systems.

Plants that are grown in lava rock or cinders are in a modified hydroponic system. They are usually started as cuttings in soil, and then the plugs are planted into the system. Since some soil is present, they are not true hydroponic systems, but do exhibit some of the same qualities. The root systems tend to be more vigorous and soil pests are usually not a problem. Watering is problematic since it is difficult to tell when the cinders are dry. Plants in lava rock tend to stay moist for long periods due to the pockets in the cinders that retain moisture and the adapted root systems.

Hydroponic Systems

Hydroponic systems are a way of growing plants without a soil medium. Some systems use LECA pebbles, others use a fibrous material such as rock wool to support the stems and give the plants an anchor. The plants must be started from seedlings

Pruning and Grooming

Above all else, people enjoy indoor plants for their visual beauty and thus appreciate plants that are fresh, clean, healthy, and growing. They notice when a plant is dirty, has yellow leaves or browned edges, or has lost its shape. Unattractive plants reflect poorly on their owners. Just one yellow leaf is all it takes for people to think that all the plants are dead, and therefore the building is falling into ruins.

Keeping plants clean, trimmed, and healthy is not difficult, but it does take time and a little effort. Grooming them regularly makes the job go faster and easier. Caring for indoor plants also maintains the safety of the interiorscape. Plants that are not watered or pruned properly may become top-heavy and topple over, posing a safety hazard. Trimming plants and keeping them pruned out of pedestrian pathways is important, especially when the plants have sharp leaves and twigs which can poke people in the face as they walk by. Healthy, pest-free plants not only look better, they also don't require the use of chemical pesticides. Clean plants breathe better and can more effectively remove toxins from the air, giving back fresh oxygen and water vapor.

Keeping plants alive and beautiful also maintains the reputation and branding of the building and indoor space. Dead and dying plants don't speak well of their owners. Patients will lose their confidence in a doctor who can't seem to keep his or her plants alive, let alone help them to stay alive and healthy. A luxury hotel doesn't look luxurious if the plants are dead. If investors and visitors see pesticides being sprayed or plastic plants in the lobby of a company that brands itself as eco-friendly, that company loses credibility. A successful corporation or financial services business does not invoke trust and confidence if it appears unable to afford healthy, fresh plants in its building.

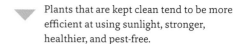

Plants that are kept clean tend to be more efficient at using sunlight, stronger, healthier, and pest-free.

CLEANING PLANTS

Clean plants are healthy plants. A plant that is cleaned frequently by wiping its leaves will have very few pest problems, since any pests are wiped off before they are noticeable. Wiping off leaves also helps keep the stomates clear so plants can breathe and so their metabolic processes can continue unabated. Clean leaves allow more light for photosynthesis. They also tend to look more green and healthy. Clean leaves show that someone cares.

Cleaning a plant's leaves is easy to do. Simply moisten a cloth and wipe the leaves from the stem end to the tip, both upper and lower sides, since most pests will hide on the undersides of leaves and most stomates are also on the undersides. Use a mild soap solution for wiping off the leaves by adding a few drops of soap in a small bucket of warm water. Avoid using antibacterial soaps, as some will damage leaves, especially in hot sunny areas. There is no need to rinse off the leaves once you wipe them. Any soap residue may help to deter pests.

To be more environmentally friendly, use a phosphate-free soap. The reason to avoid phosphate is that it acts as a fertilizer and increases the growth of algae in water sources such as ponds, choking out fish and other wildlife.

Some people prefer to use vegetable oil-based soaps, such as Castile soap or Murphy oil soap. Others prefer to use a peppermint oil–based soap; however, peppermint soaps may cause headaches and other problems for sensitive individuals. Grease-cutting soaps can help clean leaves in restaurants and other sites where the air tends to have more oil molecules, but grease-cutting soaps tend to remove some of the cuticle, the protective waxy layer on top of the epidermis of leaves, which may lead to damage in full sun. A mild liquid soap such as Ivory or one made specifically for use on babies and sensitive skin should be your first choice.

The goal should be to wash 25 to 35 percent of the leaves with each care visit, or about once every four to six weeks. If time does not permit hand wiping the leaves, spraying them with mild soapy water will help keep them looking fresh and keep pests at bay until more time is available.

Use a soft cloth to wipe leaves. If you are washing plants that have pests, use a clean paper towel for each plant and throw it out before moving onto the next plant. This will prevent the spread of pests via your wash towel from plant to plant. Otherwise, a reusable cloth can be used. Disposable products such as Handiwipes work well, hold up for a long time, and can be washed. Rags sold for mechanic shops and washing cars are another good choice. Old cotton socks have the advantage of fitting over your hand like a glove, making washing easy. Professional dusting products like Plant Paws are made specifically for plant care; they fit over your hand with the advantage of slipping up onto the forearm when not in use, and can be laundered many times. Pieces of capillary matting also can be used to wash plants.

Feather dusters and lambs' wool dusters are other tools for cleaning plants when time does not allow for wiping off individual leaves. Such products will remove any loose dust, but do not get rid of any oil build-up or other residues. Dusters should not be used on plants that are likely to have pests as the pests and their eggs will also be wiped off by the dusters and can be easily transferred from plant to plant.

REMOVING YELLOW LEAVES

Plant leaves have a limited lifespan. Some yellow and die due to wilting, lack of light, nutritional problems, disease, or pest damage. Others die simply due to old age. Whatever the reason,

Large trees will need to be cleaned during off hours when the building is closed, for safety reasons. Power pressure sprayers, ladders, and waterproof clothing may be needed.

people don't like to see plants with yellow leaves. In their minds, a single yellow leaf means that the plant is dying. In fact, one plant with one yellow leaf means that *all* of the plants in the building are dying. Therefore yellowing leaves must be removed as quickly as possible.

Yellow leaves will never green up again. Their chloroplasts have been damaged and will not recover. Pale green leaves may turn a vibrant green again, once they are watered, fertilized, or given more light, but even then, some pale leaves may continue to die and turn yellow, depending on whether or not they have been permanently damaged.

The best way to remove yellow leaves is to pull them off the stem. Dying leaves form an abscission layer (a weak layer of tissue which allows the stalk to be broken, thus shedding the leaf) of cells at the base of their petioles, near the stem, that makes pulling them off easy. Simply grasp the leaf close to the base and pull down firmly to snap it off. Holding the stem with the other hand may make this easier to do. Be sure to remove the petiole and any dying sheaths around the stem as well, since these make a plant look ugly and provide a good hiding place for pests.

If the leaf has not yet formed its abscission layer, it may be difficult to remove the leaf without causing damage to the stem. In this case, cut off the leaf as close to the stem as possible with a sharp pair of clean scissors or hand pruners. The remaining bit of petiole or sheath may be safely removed once dry.

Broad leaves can be split and torn down the middle first, then peeled away at the stem. This works well with many varieties of dracaenas, such as mass canes.

Healthy, green leaves are sometimes removed from plants to open the leaf canopy so light can penetrate to the leaves that remain. This technique will often prevent leaves from turning yellow, especially leaves on new plants, lower leaves, and those in the center of the canopy. A surprisingly large number of leaves can be removed without significantly changing the overall appearance of a full plant. Thinning plants out in this manner encourages new growth and helps a plant to acclimate to its new surroundings.

TRIMMING LEAVES

Leaves may develop yellow or brown edges and tips. This is not normal—it is a symptom of a problem, usually a nutritional imbalance or watering problem. Brown edges and tips make leaves and the plant look ugly, sickly, and dirty, even if the plant is overall clean and in good shape.

If the plant is lush and full and only a very few leaves are marred, simply remove the browned leaves. This is the fastest way to resolve this problem. However, sometimes the plant is sparse, or many of the leaves have browned edges and tips. Removing all of the leaves at one time would result in a very thinned-out plant, with only a few leaves remaining. In this case, the browning leaves should be carefully trimmed with a clean, sharp pair of scissors.

When trimming leaves, cut off the browned edges and tips to the overall natural shape of the leaf. Taking an extra couple of seconds to round off the edges at the base of the cuts will make the look seamless and more natural. The goal is to make the leaf look as though it has not been trimmed. The points should be pointed and the lower edges of the cuts should merge seamlessly into the leaf. Cut both sides of the leaf, even if the browning is only on one side, so the leaf is still symmetrical.

If the leaves are narrow and come to a sharp point, such as in a marginata, you may be able to make only one slanted cut to trim off a brown tip.

For palm fronds, cut the entire frond to the overall shape of the entire frond, rather than cutting each individual leaflet to a sharp point. This will look more natural.

 The leaves of this *Dracaena fragrans* 'Janet Craig' have been trimmed to their natural shape. It is almost impossible to tell which leaves have been trimmed.

For rhapis palms, which naturally have ragged tips, tear the leaves with your fingers as if they were made of paper. Grasp all the leaflets of a frond into a bunch, then rip off the tips of the leaflets with your fingers. This will produce a naturally ragged edge that heals better than an edge cut with scissors. Using pinking shears or zigzag craft scissors works well, too.

Be aware that the tips and edges may continue to brown after trimming if the problem still exists. The watering problem or nutritional imbalance needs to be remedied to stop the browning from continuing. A slight line of brown may develop along the edges of the cut—this is a normal part of the healing and should remain on the leaf—but any further, obvious browning will need to be trimmed again.

As a general rule, when browned tips cover more than 20 to 35 percent of a leaf, that leaf should be removed rather than trimmed, except in extreme cases. Further trimming would result in what is known as a neck-tie leaf, which looks ugly and unnatural.

Cutting Plants Back

One of the best ways to maintain the size and design integrity of a plant as well as its overall appearance is to cut the plant back on a regular basis. Cutting back refers to pruning out *green*

An old plant of *Aglaonema* 'Silver Queen'. Many of the lower leaves have been lost due to old age and inadequate light, since the lower leaves are below the windowsill and not receiving direct sunlight. In its present condition, the plant should be replaced with a new one.

This is the same plant with nearly half of its tallest stems removed. The stems were cut near the soil line, then shortened prior to planting them back in the same pot. The plant is now looking much better and can stay in its current location for months or years to come.

stems to reduce the overall size and correct the shape of a plant. Pruning refers primarily to cutting *woody* stems and branches, both for aesthetics and the health of a plant.

When cutting back stems, always cut back to another branch, twig, or leaf. That is the point where an axillary (or lateral) bud is hiding, waiting to break dormancy, pop out and start growing. Always try to cut back to within the leaf canopy, so the cut is not visible, and so additional pruning will not be required in a month or two once the stem starts growing again. It is important to cut back to a leaf or stem growing in the direction desired for new growth. Generally speaking, this means cutting back to an outward-facing leaf or stem, rather than one facing the center of the canopy (unless the canopy is sparse in the center and the goal is to fill in the center). Be sure to clean and disinfect scissors and pruners before visiting the next site, and after working on a plant with problems, to avoid spreading diseases.

When cutting back cane-form plants that have grown too tall, the heads or tufts of foliage can be cut back to within an inch or two of the main trunk. A new head of foliage will sprout out and grow within a few months, depending on the lighting.

When cutting back tall stems on shrublike plants such as arboricolas and aglaonemas, cut the stems back to within an inch or two of the soil line, preferably within the leaf canopy. This will encourage straight, new growth while hiding the cut. The new stem will grow out at an angle from the old stem in a gooseneck shape, which can look unnatural if visible to the eye.

Cuttings can often be used to grow new stems to make a sparse-looking plant full again. Shorten the cut stem if needed, strip off the foliage on the

This ficus tree was not pruned correctly. A stump was left several inches long, which looks obvious and will not heal well. Note that the bark on the remaining branch was stripped, indicating that the pruners were not sharp enough to make a clean, healthy cut.

This aglaonema was too wide, and people walking by were bruising the leaves. Several stems were cut out near the soil line to thin out the plant and bring it back to the needed size. These cuttings can now be discarded, or rooted with another aglaonema of the same variety to help make the second plant look fuller and healthier. Note that less than 30 percent of the stems were removed so the reduction would not be noticeable.

bottom, and firmly stick the cut stem into the soil. It the root ball is dense, use a soil probe or pair of scissors to dig the hole. Cuttings may also be taken to other sites that have sparse plants.

Not all plants will grow from cuttings, and plants need to have sufficient light for active growth if cuttings are to take root. Taking cuttings works especially well on most bush-type and vining plants, such as Chinese evergreens, arbori-colas, pothos, marginatas, and most dracaenas. Cuttings, however, should not be mixed with plants of different species or varieties, since this will result in a messy-looking pot of unmatched plants. Too many cuttings in one pot can also

create a plant that is too full and that cannot be matched when it is time to replace that plant.

Some indoor plants, however, should not be cut back. These include ferns, snake plants (*Sansevieria* species), some succulents, peace lilies (*Spathiphyllum* species), and solitary-trunked palms. Ferns do not have lateral buds and so will grow back from the soil but not from stems. *Sansevieria* and similar plants have underground stems or very short, compacted stems. When their leaves are removed, the stems may send out new leaves somewhere else within the pot. Spathiphyllums also have very short, compacted stems and should not be cut back, although individual leaves can be removed. Solitary-trunked palms, such as fan palms, will not grow back once they are cut and will start to die, since the single growing bud (the terminal bud) has been removed, and no lateral buds exist.

PRUNING WOODY PLANTS

Shrublike plants and trees need to be pruned occasionally to maintain the design integrity, for the health of the plant, and for safety reasons. Trees may grow so large that they become top-heavy and their shallow indoor root system is unable to hold the tree up. A tree that is ready to fall over poses a large safety risk. It will need to be pruned back and thinned out, much the same way as green-stemmed plants. Trees may also need to be cabled for additional support until the roots are able to once again support the tree in an upright position.

When pruning woody stems, use the same principles as cutting back green stems. Cut close to the main branch or trunk without leaving a stump, hiding the cut within the foliage canopy when possible. Larger branches are connected to the trunk with an overlap of woody tissue called the branch collar. This is the area where the wood of the trunk overlaps with the wood of the branch. Branches will eventually die back to the branch collar. When pruning, leave this collar intact, so no diseases are introduced into the main trunk. Always disinfect your pruners and other pruning equipment prior to working on indoor plants and trees.

REMOVING LARGE PALM FRONDS

Large palm fronds, especially fan-shaped fronds, can be very heavy and pose a serious safety risk. They should be removed before they fall off on their own. Only a licensed arborist should do this work on specimen palms over 12 feet in height. Many people have been seriously injured by large fronds falling onto them. Although this rarely happens on indoor plants, special precautions by experts must be taken to protect both workers and the general public.

12 Plant Problems

Indoor plants are not growing under ideal conditions. They rarely get enough light. Frequently the substrate in which they grow is a concocted medium that contains no actual "soil." They rely on fertilizers for nutrients rather than composting organic matter found in nature. They do not get a regular bath from rainfall to wash away pests. Yet, indoors they are highly visible and in close proximity to their owners and visitors, who demand unrealistic standards of perfection, unlike their counterparts growing outdoors.

Indoor plants, at one time or another in their lives, will most likely develop problems. These problems include those caused by nutrient imbalances, pests, diseases, and environmental issues. Prevention is key to controlling these issues and keeping any problems under control. It is far less time consuming and less expensive to prevent problems from developing in the first place than it is to try and treat problems once they occur.

Prevention is centered on good design choices and horticultural practices, as has been discussed throughout this book. These include providing adequate lighting and choosing plants that will do best in the light conditions available, watering correctly, cleaning and grooming plants regularly, following a well-developed fertilization and nutritional monitoring program, practicing good horticultural hygiene, such as disinfecting tools, and acting quickly when a problem does occur.

Frequently when a plant has a problem, more than one issue is involved. A plant with an environmental problem is more prone to develop a disease in its weakened condition. Pests can easily transmit diseases

Faint yellow splotches on leaves are often the first sign of fluoride toxicity, which can happen when levels of fluoride in the tap water are very high. Fluoride toxicity can also occur when a plant becomes too dry. Since fluoride is not available to plants at higher pH levels, the addition of dolomitic lime in the soil can help.

from one plant to the next. Some diseases occur as secondary infections after another disease has taken hold. All of the problems need to be addressed simultaneously to bring a sick plant back to health.

NUTRITIONAL IMBALANCES

Nutritional plant problems are very common and often overlooked. Symptoms may mimic diseases or watering problems and be treated incorrectly. Some people may think that foliage with brown edges and tips or other discolorations are "normal" and overlook the underlying issue because they don't know what a healthy plant looks like.

Nutritional problems can be broken down into two categories: nutrient toxicities (too much) or nutrient deficiencies (too little). Some nutrient problems are the result of improper watering. For example, plants that dry out too much can easily develop soluble salts damage as well as fluoride

and boron toxicities. On the other extreme, plants that are kept too wet can develop nitrogen deficiency when the microbes in soil that help a plant take up nitrogen drown in the overly wet soil medium.

The pH level (the level of acidity or alkalinity) in a soil medium can also lead to nutrient problems, particularly iron deficiency. The various minerals and nutrients that a plant requires are available to plants at different pH levels—some at more acidic levels (pH below 7.0) and some at more alkaline levels (pH above 7.0). Most of the minerals a plant needs are available at pH levels between 6.5 and 6.8 in slightly acidic soils.

When pH levels are significantly higher or lower, nutrient deficiencies may result. This frequently happens over time in cities where the pH levels of water are high due to the minerals in the outdoor soil. In such cities, a buffer may need to be added to water to correct the pH. When watering indoor plants, it may help to use an acidic fertilizer, such as those made for azaleas or African violets. Most soil media contain peat and are already slightly acidic, but pH levels can change over time as the peat decomposes and water alters the level of the soil pH.

Nutrient toxicity usually occurs as soluble salts toxicity, a build-up in the soil of excess fertilizer salts caused by overfertilizing or allowing a plant to dry out too much. The toxicity tends to occur on newer leaves and newer plants. Roots may be burned by the build-up of salts in the soil as water is drawn *out* of the root cells instead of *into* the root cells. Excess salts can lead to overall wilting and death of the plant in extreme cases. More often, the excess salts are taken up into the plant and pushed outward through the stomates found at the tips and edges of the leaves. This dehydrates and kills the cells along the leaf edges and tips, causing the browning so often seen on plant leaves.

Soluble salts toxicity is best prevented by proper watering techniques, removal of any visible time-release fertilizer pellets, and leaching plants when they are first delivered to the greenhouse. Leaching the soil may help to relieve soluble salts build-up by flushing the excess salts out of the soil.

Boron toxicity occurs primarily on *Dracaena deremensis* 'Warneckii' and is indicated by brown spots with a yellowish halo, often accompanied by browned edges and tips on the leaves. This can easily be confused with a leafspot disease. A soil test may be needed.

Nutrient deficiencies tend to occur on older leaves and older plants. Most susceptible are mature plants that have not been fertilized for some time. An overall yellowing or pale green coloring, and slow or stalled growth, are the most frequent symptoms. Iron and manganese deficiencies show up as yellowing between the leaf veins (interveinal chlorosis), which remain green.

Calcium and boron deficiencies are indicated by bent stems and frond midribs and are most often seen on palms.

Palms are notorious for developing nutrient deficiency problems because their vascular system (the tissues that transport water and nutrients) are scattered (discontinuous), which makes taking up nutrients from the soil more difficult for them than for plants with a ringlike (continuous) vascular system. A closely monitored fertilization program is highly recommended for palms.

Macronutrients and Micronutrients

Plants need six minerals in higher quantities (the macronutrients) and a number of nutrients in smaller quantities (the micronutrients). The "big three" are nitrogen, phosphorous, and potassium, which are included in most fertilizers. Even though some nutrients are needed in smaller quantities, they are very important to the health and metabolic processes of a plant. In fact, most nutrient deficiencies are caused by lack of a micronutrient, not a macronutrient.

The roles of macronutrients and micronutrients are very complex. They are components of cellular structures in plants, such as chlorophyll, cell walls, cell membranes, energy-storing compounds, and enzymes. They also play important roles in the life-sustaining activities of plants such as opening and closing stomates, activating enzymes, utilizing other nutrients, and the process of photosynthesis.

Fertilizers

Numerous fertilizers have been formulated to provide plants with the nutrients they need to remain healthy. A complete fertilizer is one in which all of the nutrients, both macronutrients and micronutrients, are provided. Complete fertilizers are recommended particularly for palms (which suffer from nutrient deficiencies) and plants that have been on a site for a long time, depleting the micronutrients usually present in most soil media. Specialized complete fertilizers are available for plants grown in hydroponics. Other fertilizers are targeted to a particular crop of plants, such as poinsettias, azaleas, or orchids, to address their specific needs.

The three numbers found on every fertilizer label indicate the percentage of active ingredients for the "big three" macronutrients: nitrogen (N), phosphorous (P), and potassium (K), in that order. A fertilizer labeled as 15–30–15 would have 15 percent nitrogen, 30 percent phosphorous, and 15 percent potassium active ingredients, with a total of 60 percent active ingredients. A 1–2–1 fertilizer would have the same ratio of these nutrients, but in much smaller amounts, with a total of only 4 percent active ingredients.

Many organic fertilizers have smaller amounts of active ingredients. Organic fertilizers are not necessarily better for plant growth. They are often more diluted and may not be as cost effective, especially if large amounts are needed. In addition, many organic fertilizers include bone meal, dried blood, fish emulsion, and other components that give off a noticeable and undesirable odor, making them a poor choice in an enclosed indoor space. Most organic fertilizers, however, are more eco-friendly, emitting fewer toxins into the air, and using agricultural by-products that are readily available and sustainable.

The other nutrients included in a fertilizer are identified with their percentage of active ingredients in the list of contents on the label. The amounts are usually much smaller, frequently a percentage of 1 percent. Nonetheless, such small quantities of nutrients make a large difference to the health of a plant.

Most professionals recommend a 24–8–16 fertilizer for indoor plants (or one with a 3–1–2 ratio). A 20–20–20 fertilizer, or a 15–30–15 fertilizer, are considered good all-purpose fertilizers and can also be used on indoor plants.

Micronutrient deficiencies can also be remedied by using a fertilizer with only that particular micronutrient in a formula that is readily available for a plant. For example, chelated iron can be used by itself to resolve an iron deficiency.

Most fertilizers are somewhat acidic, which assists in the uptake of nutrients, particularly the micronutrients. If the soil is too alkaline, a more acidic fertilizer can be used to lower the pH, such as one formulated for azaleas or other acid-loving plants. On the rare occasions when a soil is too acidic, dolomitic or agricultural lime can be added to the soil to adjust the pH.

PESTS

Both indoor and outdoor plants are prone to attack by insects and other pests. Outdoor plants rely on natural predators and parasites to eat the pests, and rainfall to wash pests off. Indoor plants must rely on people to effectively control pests.

Inspecting plants when they are first delivered is very important in keeping pest populations

Take a close look at this leaf. The dusty, pinpricked look is a result of spider mites feeding on the lower surface.

under control. Pests can easily be brought in by new plants, including those that employees bring in from home, and will spread quickly to healthy, established plants. Pests are spread via tools, clothing, equipment, and through the air. Many pests are mobile and can fly or crawl from one plant to another on their own. People can brush up against a plant, pick up a few insect eggs, and deposit them back onto the next plant they brush up against, all without realizing what has happened.

Many pests are quite small and require a keen eye and the knowledge of what each stage looks like. Eggs, larval, pupal, and adult stages can look quite different from each other. Many pesticides only work on the larval or pupal stages, so early detection is very important.

Keeping plants clean and frequently wiping the leaves will control most pests in their early stages. Regularly cleaning and disinfecting tools will also help. As a precaution, many companies will apply a preventative treatment on plants before they are delivered to their final home.

The most common pests on indoor plants include spider mites, mealybugs, aphids, scale, fungus gnats, whitefly, and thrips. Occasionally problems occur with banana moths, cockroaches, and other pests.

Spider Mites

Mites belong to the spider family and have eight legs (unlike an insect which has six) and a piercing, sucking mouthpart. The most common type of mite on indoor plants is the two-spotted spider mite (*Tetranychus urticae*). It has two large spots on its reddish back and is about the size of a typed period or pencil mark. Its eggs look like a fine, rust-colored dust. Two-spotted mites usually attack plants that are in hot, sunny, dry areas, especially ferns and marginatas. They prefer plants with thin, papery leaves.

Spider mites lay about 100 eggs at a time and mature in 7 to 10 days. If a plant starts out with one mite (highly possible) and is ignored, not cleaned or treated, the plant could have over 13 million mites within a month's time and would most likely be dead. Quick detection and control are very important where mites are concerned.

Spider mites will stick their needlelike mouths into a cell, secrete a toxic enzyme that dissolves the contents of the cell, and suck up the contents to digest. The toxic enzyme kills that cell, along with some of the surrounding cells. The damage starts out looking like pinpricked marks, as if the plant were dusty. The dead cells become dried out and blonde-colored until the entire leaf dries. Leaves may feel gritty (the eggs and dead bodies of the mites).

Spider mites spin fine webs along the leaves and between leaves to move and find new eating sites. The webbing also helps to protect the mites from pesticides, as droplets are caught in the webs without touching the mites. Most pesticides kill only the pupal stages and adults, not the eggs, so repeated applications at one-week intervals for a minimum of two months are necessary to bring mites under control.

Another group of mites, the eriophyids, sometimes attack yucca plants and are so small they look like powdery mildew instead of a pest. Under a magnifying glass, they look like tiny granules of rice with short, thin legs.

Spider mites are very tiny and have eight legs. Their bodies may be almost transparent when they are young.

Mealybugs often hide on the undersides of leaves and look like small bits of cotton.

 Cryptolaemus montrouzieri is a type of lady beetle that is very effective in controlling citrus mealybugs. The adults and larvae will eat mealybugs without damaging plants. Their larvae look like large, hairy mealybugs and these are best used in atriums and larger plantings.

Mealybugs

Mealybugs look like bits of cotton and may be confused with a fungus or bits of lint. The young are pinkish or orange before they develop a thick, waxy coat of cottony filaments that helps to protect them. Eggs are laid in nests of cottony fiber, usually in leaf axils, and hatch within a week or two. The young go through several larval cycles before becoming adults. The six legs are hidden beneath their bodies and can be seen by gently flipping a mealybug onto its back (they don't like that and will flop themselves back over again).

Mealybugs also have piercing, sucking mouth parts. They attack almost any plant, including cacti, and become more active as the temperature increases. They are able to crawl quickly from one plant to another and are easily transferred on clothing or through the air. Mealybugs can be seen walking across carpets, sidewalks, furniture, and walls, looking for a new home.

Several types of mealybugs attack indoor plants. The citrus mealybug (*Planococcus citri*) is the most common one and has a blunt-shaped, cottony body about the size of a pencil eraser. The long-tailed mealybug (*Pseudococcus longispinus*) has several long filaments on the end of its body and is extremely difficult to control due to a very fast life cycle. At one time long-tailed mealybugs were thought to give birth to live young, but scientists recently discovered that they do lay eggs which hatch very rapidly.

Root mealybugs (*Rhizoecus* species) live in the soil and feed on plant roots, often remaining undetected. Coconut mealybug (*Nipaecoccus nipae*) tends to be flatter and more yellow-green and is a serious problem on crops in Hawaii as well as a common pest of indoor palms.

Aphids

The aphids that most commonly attack indoor plants are light green and pear-shaped, often turning darker as they age and feed. Aphids, known in Great Britain as greenflies, blackflies, or whiteflies, give birth to about 30 live young at a time and are born already pregnant. Their life cycle is very short, and they give birth after 3 to 5 days. They also have piercing mouth parts, but their mouths are delicate as they prefer to feed on tender new growth.

Aphids are most commonly found on the new leaflets of arboricola and ming aralia, particularly when the plants are grown in hot sunny windows. These pests also feed on flowers, especially mums. Their bodies are about the size of a printed dash (-) and they have six legs. They frequently have two abdominal tubes that look like exhaust pipes on the ends of their bodies, from which they excrete honeydew, a sticky substance that is basically plant sap that has been forced through their bodies.

Aphids are not strong enough to suck out plant juices. Instead, the turgor pressure within plant cells forces fluids up into the bodies of aphids as they feed. They tend to become bloated, looking fat and juicy, as a result of feeding. Since their bodies are translucent, they may take on the color of what they are feeding on, remaining a pale green if feeding on white flowers, or becoming dark-colored if feeding on dark leaves.

Aphids are notorious for spreading diseases and are a serious problem for greenhouse growers. Keeping plants clean will help to control aphids. Many pesticides are effective since aphid bodies are delicate and they give birth to live young instead of eggs.

The larva of a green lacewing (*Chrysoperla rufilabris*) is eating a young, almost transparent aphid. Older aphids usually become darker as they feed.

Lacewing adults will also feed on aphids, as well as most soft-bodied insects.

Scales

Many types of scales tend to attack indoor plants. They are categorized as hard-bodied (having a hard, protective shell) and soft-bodied. Soft scales excrete honeydew, which is often the first sign of their presence. Scales reproduce slowly, with a three-month life cycle or more, but are difficult to see. They look like small bumps on leaves and twigs and can be mistaken for lenticels (raised pores) and normal parts of a plant.

Most scale insects are female and are capable of reproducing without males, which look like tiny gnats and can on occasion be seen swarming around female scales on a plant. The female lays her eggs underneath her body where they eventually hatch, looking like a fine orange dust. The eggs grow and eventually consume the mother's body, then crawl out from underneath and start exploring. They mature and find a good place to eat, usually a plant vein, which their piercing mouth part will puncture so they can suck out the sap. Eventually they become permanently attached to their feeding site and lose their legs. Live scales are difficult to remove by pushing with a cloth or fingernail, whereas dead scales are easy to flick or wipe off.

Scales attack almost any plant and are often found on ficus trees, cacti, and marginatas. The latter tend to get Florida red scale (*Chrysomphalus aonidum*), which remains mobile throughout its life span, crawling slowly along a leaf, leaving a short trail of yellowed plant tissue behind.

Few pesticides work well on scale due to their protective shells and the fact that the eggs and young are kept hidden under the mother's body. Treatments must be kept up for several months to catch all of the generations of scale. Physical removal takes time and usually damages the leaves. Pruning off infected leaves and branches is usually best if the infestation is not too serious.

Fungus Gnats

Fungus gnats are tiny insects about the same size as a fruit fly. Their bodies are slim and narrow with dark-veined wedge-shaped wings and long slender legs. They breed in moist, overwatered soil media with high organic content and are nuisance pests, often flying into people's faces. They are most likely the number one complaint that people have concerning their indoor plants. Eventually gnats damage plant roots as they feed on dead and dying organic matter. They are attracted to light and can be found flying around windows. They are also attracted to fruits and sweet liquids, similar to fruit flies, making their control difficult in offices and lunchroom areas.

Fungus gnats live for about three weeks and lay their eggs in the top layers of the soil medium. The eggs hatch into tiny wormlike larvae that are nearly transparent with dark-colored heads. The larvae feed in the soil until they pupate and hatch into the adult gnats, which will often fly onto other plants and can quickly spread throughout an office area.

The easiest way to control fungus gnats is by watering plants properly, avoiding the use of a high-peat soil medium, and controlling the larval stages in the medium. Many methods work, provided they are applied for several months to catch all of the generations of fungus gnats. These methods include mixing sand or diatomaceous earth into the soil to slice up the larvae and deter egg laying, applying various chemical pesticides to the soil, and using predatory mite species specifically targeted to control fungus gnats.

Placing yellow sticky cards or slices of raw potato on the soil surface will help to capture adults and larva to determine which plants are infested. However, this is not an effective means of capturing and killing all of the pests and should be used solely for detection purposes.

Note that pests that attack plants will not bite people. Their mouth parts are too delicate to pierce human skin. Some people may be allergic to certain insects, especially if the saliva comes in contact with their skin, and they may feel itchy. Most of the time, anyone who thinks they've been bitten by a plant pest has been bitten by something else.

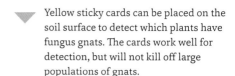

Yellow sticky cards can be placed on the soil surface to detect which plants have fungus gnats. The cards work well for detection, but will not kill off large populations of gnats.

Other Pests

True whiteflies (not to be confused with their close relatives the aphids) are rare on indoor plants, but may attack poinsettias during the holiday season and some indoor flowering plants. They look like small white moths and often rest on the undersides of leaves. Since most flowering plants are seasonal in nature, it is best to discard any infested plants before the whiteflies move on to attack other plants in the area.

Thrips occasionally attack *Ficus nitida* trees in the interiorscape. The larva make newer leaves curl tightly into a closed envelope and are easily seen once the leaves are forced open. They may also attack flowering plants such as mums and peace lily flowers. The adults are rapid flyers and can travel quickly from one plant to another, laying their eggs on the leaves or dropping to the soil to lay their eggs. Pick off affected plant parts to control this occasional pest, which can spread diseases.

Within the past few years banana moths have become a problem on *Dracaena fragrans* 'Massangeana' canes and bamboo palms. The larvae get into the stems and eat their way through, causing serious damage. Once they are in their final stages, they bore their way out of the canes and fly off as moths, leaving sawdust and damaged canes behind. Most often the plants are infested at the nursery, and damage may not be apparent for several months until the moths emerge from the canes. Severe damage can cause death to infested plants.

Cockroaches are not really plant pests; they are classified as structural pests. However, they frequently burrow into the top dressing and soil medium where they will breed and damage roots. Cockroaches are usually a problem in shopping malls where roaches will often find their way into garden plantings, but they can occur in the best of offices and other sites.

Cockroaches usually occur in colonies, even if you only see one insect. If only one plant is infested, it should be discarded. If applying pesticides or roach baits, control efforts should be coordinated with building's extermination vendor so the roaches do not travel back and forth from the plants to building crevices, and back again during pesticide applications.

Beneficial Insects and Other Organisms

Indoor pests in garden atriums, along with certain soil-borne pests, can be controlled by using beneficial insects, mites, and other living organisms. Most beneficials are very small and unnoticeable to the public. Using beneficials is more eco-friendly and cost-effective, since only one or two applications per season are usually needed.

Beneficials give the best results in garden plantings, as opposed to container plants, since the pest population will usually be large enough to support the beneficials and provide them with enough food to survive. Some states require a pesticide applicator license and/or permit to use beneficials and other nonchemical means of pest control, so check with the local state agriculture extension office prior to using them commercially.

Most beneficials can be classified as predators or parasites. Predators eat the pests—the adults, eggs, larva, or some combination. Many attack a specific pest, such as mealybug ladybird (*Cryptolaemus montrouzieri*) which attacks mealybugs. Others attack a wider variety of pests. For example, lacewings attack almost any soft-bodied pest, including aphids and mealybugs. Beneficial mites may attack pest mites or fungus gnats, depending on the genus. Beneficial nematodes attack fungus gnat larva and are often sold as a pesticide.

Beneficials have very specific needs of temperature and humidity to do their best work. An insectary (a commercial business which raises beneficial insects and mites to sell) can recommend the best option. The beneficials may be sold as eggs, larva, or adults. They should be applied as soon after delivery as possible, preferably in the cool of the morning or evening, for best results.

If applying beneficials to the leaf canopy, first spray some sugar water onto the plants to provide water and nutrition for beneficials until they crawl or fly and find their target pests.

Chemical Pesticides

There are many chemical pesticides labelled for indoor use on plants, and the labels and application requirements may change frequently. Most states have laws and regulations governing the use of chemicals for pest control, especially when the person and business are being paid to apply them. This includes pesticides that can be purchased at retail stores. Always check with your state extension office to see what restrictions and regulations are in place.

When choosing a chemical pesticide, look for the safest option, preferably a pesticide with the word *caution* on the label. The word *warning* indicates a pesticide that is more toxic, and additional safety precautions will be required. The words *danger–poison* indicate the most toxic pesticides, and these should not be used indoors.

Also check the label to make sure that the pest you want to control is listed on it, and that the label states "for indoor use," "for interior plantscapes," or something similar. If the plants you are treating are not on the label, you run a certain amount of risk that the pesticide may cause harm to the plants, especially if they are located in a hot, sunny area.

Be sure to follow all of the safety precautions, including clean-up and storage, and read the entire label before using. Follow state regulations concerning record-keeping and make sure your license and permits are kept up to date.

DISEASES

From time to time, an indoor plant will suffer from a disease, which can be transmitted to the plant via several routes. Pests can spread diseases, especially those with piercing mouth parts such as mites and aphids. Pathogens (disease-causing organisms such as bacteria or fungi) may be passed on via tools such as pruners, scissors, and soil probes that were used on an infected plant and not disinfected. Pathogens can also enter a plant through leaf stomates or any cuts when water from an infected plant is splashed onto a healthy one. Other pathogens found in the soil can enter through the plant's roots or be splashed onto the foliage.

Often plant diseases occur along with other plant problems, such as pests, physical damage, overwatering, nutritional imbalances, poor lighting, and any conditions that weaken indoor plants. These added problems must be resolved as well as the disease to bring a plant back to a healthy condition.

Plant diseases on indoor plants are primarily caused by fungi and bacteria. Most plant diseases caused by viruses are controlled at the greenhouse and nursery and never make it to the interior plantscape. Fungi and bacteria attack plants only and not people. Diseases need a susceptible host in order to develop. Therefore, a leafspot disease will not develop in a human, and a plant will never get the measles or flu.

Most plant diseases that attack indoor plants are not well-controlled by fungicides or bactericides, and very few chemicals for plant disease control are labelled for use in the interior plantscape. Infected plant parts, such as stems or leaves, should be removed as quickly as possible to prevent the spread of disease, and any tools disinfected prior to working on the next plant. Preventive methods include proper care, good watering practices, and pest control.

Because many plant diseases are specific to the type of plant or genus that they will attack, they are fairly easy to diagnose once they are detected. Most plant diseases on indoor plants are fungal leafspot diseases. These are usually characterized by a brown or reddish-brown spot with a yellowish halo. Fusarium attacks dracaenas and other plants. When it infects palms and *Ficus* 'Alii', it sometimes appears as yellow to brown splotches. Anthracnose infects aglaonemas, dracaenas, and other plants. Helminthosporium causes leafspot on palms while coniothyrium causes black spots on yucca.

Other fungal diseases include rhizoctonia, which causes rotting on pothos and other ground-cover plants; it often begins in the soil. Phomopsis produces dieback disease (death of twigs and branches) on ficus trees. Sooty mold is a black fungus that grows on top of honeydew, a sugary substance secreted by aphids and other plant pests.

Root rot diseases usually occur on newer plants and those that are sitting in water. They include phytophthora and its close relative pythium, both of which attack pothos and other plants.

Bacterial diseases attack plants that have been overwatered, especially those that have been sitting in water for long periods. They may occur along with root rot diseases. Two of the most common bacterial diseases are erwinia and xanthomonas. Erwinia causes a smelly, watery rot of roots, leaves, and stems, especially on some *Philodendron* species and on aglaonemas. Xanthomonas causes leafspots similar to fungal leafspots.

ENVIRONMENTAL PROBLEMS

The environment itself can create problems for plants, besides those caused by watering and lighting issues. Most environmental problems can be prevented, and control is easy if the environment itself can be altered.

Epinasty (increased growth on the upper surface of a plant part) occurs primarily on poinsettias and causes permanent wilting and drooping of leaves and stems. Most plants, including flowering plants and ripening fruit, give off ethylene gas. If kept in closed boxes for too long, the ethylene gas builds up and causes wilting and drooping that is often irreversible. Poinsettias and other sensitive plants should be opened and taken out of their boxes as quickly as possible. Avoid storing ripening fruit in an enclosed space, such as a flower cooler, if plants or flowers are also stored in the space.

Chill damage can occur on tropical and subtropical indoor plants if the temperatures drop below 45 to 55 degrees Fahrenheit, especially for long periods of time. Damage can also occur if very cold water is used, especially on more sensitive plants such as *Aglaonema*. The damage may appear as a mottled or mosaic discoloring on foliage, as root and bud damage, or as flowering on foliage plants such as dracaenas.

Cold damage occurs in freezing temperatures of 32 degrees Fahrenheit or below. Leaves, stems, and roots become dark, watery, and wet, eventually rotting away. Cold damage is often fatal.

Although not well-studied, plants seem to react negatively to chlorine vapors in the air around indoor pools and large fountains. Plants may become discolored and wilted, and new growth ceases. The plants seem to slowly decline and develop a "failure to thrive." Minerals from splashing water may encrust the leaves, causing an unsightly mess and interfering with stomate activity and photosynthesis in severe cases. Expect to replace plants more frequently in these locations.

In conclusion, most plants will grow healthy and strong with very few, if any, pest and disease problems if proper horticultural practices are used. Proper watering and grooming, preferably by an experienced professional horticulturist, will prevent most problems before they occur while keeping indoor plants looking their best for years to come.

13 The Plant Palette

Every good painter has a palette of colors for mixing and creating a work of art. Horticulturists and designers have a palette of indoor plants to choose from for their work of art, too. An artist doesn't need every color under the rainbow to create a masterpiece—in fact, many artists work with a limited palette of five or six colors on any one painting. The same advice can be applied to designing the interiorscape—a few carefully chosen plants will have more impact than a "one-of-each" approach.

This chapter describes the most commonly used indoor plants for commercial spaces, with their varieties and variations. For a design to be successful over the long term, the designer should keep in mind the lighting requirements as well as the shape and size of the plants selected.

The information included here is based on the author's personal experience and on national standards. Please note that some plants may have more than one common name and more than one botanical name. The most commonly accepted names have been used, including those cited in the 5th edition of *The Guide to Interior Landscape Specifications* (2003), published by ALCA (now National Association of Landscape Professionals).

Lighting key

Low light	30 to 100 FC	mostly artificial light
Low to medium light	50 to 150 FC	mostly artificial light
Medium light	150 to 200 FC	mostly artificial light, possibly some indirect sunlight
Bright indirect light	175 to 225 FC	indirect sunlight
Bright light	200 to 250 FC	direct sunlight 2 to 4 hours per day
High light	250+ FC	direct sunlight at least 6 hours per day

FOLIAGE PLANTS

Adonidia palm

Adonidia merrillii

DESIGN USE Atriums, gardens

SHAPES Solitary-trunked palm with arching fronds at top

HEIGHT/POT SIZE 6 feet tall in 14-inch pot, up to specimen size

LIGHTING High light

WATERING Keep moist

COMMENTS A relatively inexpensive palm for its size. Susceptible to spider mites in high light. Usually sold with multiple trunks in the same pot.

Amstel King ficus

Ficus binnendijkii 'Amstel King'

DESIGN USE Floor plant, gardens, atriums, patioscapes

SHAPES Usually a tree form

HEIGHT/POT SIZE 4 to 5 feet tall in 10-inch pot, up to 12 feet in 21-inch pot

LIGHTING Bright indirect light to high light

WATERING Keep moist

COMMENTS Has strappy leaves. 'Amstel King' is considered hardier than 'Alii' and has replaced it for most projects.

Arboricola, Arb, Umbrella plant, Miniature schefflera, Hawaiian schefflera

Schefflera arboricola

DESIGN USE Floor plant, desktop plant, dish gardens, green walls, gardens

SHAPES May be grown as a round bush or trimmed into a topiary tree shape

HEIGHT/POT SIZE 6-inch plant in 4-inch pot, up to 6- to 8-foot tree in 17-inch pot. Bush forms are usually 2 to 4 feet tall.

LIGHTING Low to medium light

WATERING Allow to dry out somewhat between waterings

COMMENTS Related to schefflera (*Schefflera actinophylla*). Has clusters of very small leaves on a short petiole. Resembles an outdoor shrub or tree.

Areca palm

Dypsis lutescens
Synonym *Chyrsalidocarpus lutescens*

DESIGN USE Floor plant, gardens, atriums, special occasion rentals

SHAPES Fan shaped with multiple stems or fronds growing from the soil

HEIGHT/POT SIZE 4 to 5 feet tall in 10-inch pot, up to 10 feet in 17-inch pot

LIGHTING Bright indirect light. Tolerates lower light levels for short periods.

WATERING Keep moist at all times

COMMENTS Does best with some sunlight. The base of the frond is naturally speckled and turns yellow-orange in higher light levels. An inexpensive palm for its size.

Often used for rentals. Prone to spider mites and fungal leafspot diseases.

Bamboo palm

Chamaedorea erumpens or
C. 'Florida Hybrid'

DESIGN USE Floor plant, atriums

SHAPES Columnar

HEIGHT/POT SIZE 4 to 5 feet tall in 10-inch pot, up to 6 to 8 feet in 17-inch pot

LIGHTING Medium light. Tolerates lower light levels.

WATERING Allow to dry between waterings

COMMENTS Frequently used in offices since it doesn't take up much space and tolerates lower light levels. Most bamboo palms are sold as 'Florida Hybrid', a cross between *Chamaedorea erumpens* and *C. seifrizii* (reed palm). 'Florida Hybrid' creates a fuller look in a container than either parent species does and is the most common form of bamboo palm. Another species, *C. metallica* (miniature fishtail), has a natural metallic gray sheen and very wide leaflets, stays short, and is used mostly for accent or novelty.

Bird of paradise

Strelitzia nicolai

DESIGN USE Floor plant, atriums

SHAPES Fan shaped

HEIGHT/POT SIZE 4 to 5 feet in 10-inch pot, up to specimen size of 20+ feet, usually 6 to 8 feet tall 14- to 17-inch pots

LIGHTING High light

WATERING Allow to dry somewhat between waterings

COMMENTS Has white flowers and is the bird of paradise used most often in the interiorscape. Will bloom if there is sufficient light and if evenings are cool. Used primarily for its foliage and may be mistaken for a palm by unknowing visitors.

Bird's nest fern

Asplenium nidus

DESIGN USE Desktop plant, containers, gardens, patioscapes, green walls

SHAPES Fan shaped

HEIGHT/POT SIZE 8 inches tall in 6-inch pots, up to 2 to 3 feet tall in 14-inch pot, depending on the variety

LIGHTING Medium light

WATERING Keep evenly moist

COMMENTS Used frequently in green walls for its strappy leaves. Many different varieties available.

Black olive tree

Bucida buceras

DESIGN USE Atriums, gardens

SHAPES Tree shaped

HEIGHT/POT SIZE 6 to 8 feet tall in 17-inch pot, up specimen trees 20+ feet tall

LIGHTING High light is best. Acclimates to bright indirect light

WATERING Keep moist at all times

COMMENTS Almost always grown as a specimen tree. Drops all its leaves when first installed and as it acclimates. Many tiny leaves on dark branches give it a lacy effect.

Boston fern

Nephrolepis exaltata 'Bostoniensis'

DESIGN USE Desktop plant, gardens, green walls, patioscapes, special occasion rentals

SHAPES Fan shaped

HEIGHT/POT SIZE 8 to 24 inches tall in 6- to 14-inch pots

LIGHTING Bright indirect light

WATERING Keep evenly moist

COMMENTS Delicate and easily damaged. Tends to create quite a mess when the leaflets drop so not used frequently in the interiorscape except in green walls and rentals. Many different types of ferns exist but only a few are used in commercial settings, including 'Kimberly Queen' (*Nephrolepis obliterata*), also known as erect sword fern.

Cast-iron plant

Aspidistra elatior

DESIGN USE Floor plant

SHAPES Spear shaped with underground stem

HEIGHT/POT SIZE 18 to 24 inches tall in 6- to 17-inch pot

LIGHTING Low light

WATERING Allow to dry somewhat between waterings

COMMENTS Does quite well in low light but may burn if the light is too strong or if it dries out completely. Most forms have solid green leaves, although some varieties may have white spots or yellow-green to white stripes.

Chinese evergreen

Aglaonema varieties

DESIGN USE Desktop plant, short floor plant, green walls

SHAPES Mostly grown rounded

HEIGHT/POT SIZE 12 to 24 inches tall in 6-inch pot, up to 30 inches in 17-inch pot

LIGHTING Low light

WATERING Allow to dry between waterings

COMMENTS Many new varieties are available with beautiful silver or cream variegation. A few have red or pink variegation, but these require far more light. Favorites include 'Maria' (replaces 'Emerald Beauty'), 'Maria Christina', 'Silver Bay', and 'Silver Queen'.

Creeping fig

Ficus pumila

Synonym *Ficus repens*

DESIGN USE Groundcover, dish gardens, miniature gardens, terrariums, green walls

SHAPES Vining

HEIGHT/POT SIZE Stays close to the soil line, 2 inches tall, usually in 6-inch pot

LIGHTING Low to medium light

WATERING Keep somewhat moist. Tends to have a delicate root system close to the surface.

COMMENTS Strictly used as a ground cover or filler.

Croton

Codiaeum variegatum

DESIGN USE Desktop plant, floor plant, gardens, focal points, as a substitute for blooming plants and in color rotations, focal points in atrium gardens, green walls

SHAPES Spear shaped to rounded

HEIGHT/POT SIZE From small 8- to 10-inch plants in 6-inch pots to 3-foot floor plants in 17-inch pots

LIGHTING Bright direct light. Tolerates lower light levels.

WATERING Keep evenly moist

COMMENTS Known for their brightly colored foliage in variegations of yellow, orange, red, green, and purple, depending on the variety. Leaves are spoon- or oakleaf-shaped and grow on slender stems. Prone to spider mites and other problems, especially in hot sunny windows. Cultivars include 'Norma' (see photo), 'Oakleaf' (named for the shape of its foliage), and 'Petra'.

Dumbcane

Dieffenbachia species and varieties

Design use Primarily as a substitute for flowering plants in color rotations, occasionally as a desktop plant, short floor plant, in dish gardens, and in green walls

Shapes Spear shaped, fan shaped, or rounded

Height/Pot size 6 inches tall in 4-inch pot, to 3 feet tall in 10-inch pot

Lighting Bright indirect light

Watering Keep fairly moist. Allow to dry out just slightly between waterings.

Comments Brightly variegated leaves with white markings, dependent on the variety. Very prone to spider mites and other problems. Not commonly used today in commercial interiorscapes except as a substitute for blooming plants in color rotations. Sap can cause irritation. Common forms include 'Amoena' (dark green leaves with white diagonal striping), 'Camille' (creamy yellow leaves with green edge), 'Compacta' (cream leaves with green mottling, compact habit), and 'Tropic Snow' (dark green leaves with white blotches; see photo).

English ivy

Hedera helix

Design use Desktop plant, dish gardens, hanging basket, groundcover, filler in container gardens and patioscapes, green walls

Shapes Vining

Height/Pot size Stays low, 6 inches tall in 4- to 10-inch pot

Lighting Bright indirect light

Watering Allow to dry between waterings

Comments Susceptible to spider mites in hot sunny areas. Hundreds of varieties are available, some with yellow or white variegation. Leaf size varies with the variety. The most popular indoor varieties include 'Glacier' (strong white variegation), 'Needlepoint' (small narrow leaves with white variegation; see photo), and *Hedera algeriensis* (large flat green leaves).

Fiddleleaf fig

Ficus lyrata

DESIGN USE Floor plant, atriums, gardens

SHAPES Usually a fan-shaped tree with cascading branches

HEIGHT/POT SIZE 5 to 6 feet tall in 14-inch pot, up to specimen size

LIGHTING Bright indirect light to high light

WATERING Keep moist except in lower light levels

COMMENTS Does best with some sunlight. Very broad, flat leaves give this plant a rough texture.

Fishtail palm

Caryota mitis

DESIGN USE Floor plant, atriums, gardens

SHAPES Columnar with arching fronds

HEIGHT/POT SIZE 6 feet tall in 14-inch pot, up to 15-foot specimen

LIGHTING Bright indirect light. Tolerates lower light levels.

WATERING Keep moist at all times. Do not allow to dry out.

COMMENTS Fishtail palm will die if it is allowed to dry out, especially during the first few weeks after it is delivered. Susceptible to spider mites in sunny locations.

Heart-leaf philodendron

Philodendron cordatum

DESIGN USE Desktop plant, dish gardens, miniature gardens, green walls

SHAPES Vining

HEIGHT/POT SIZE Vine in 2- to 6-inch pot

LIGHTING Low light

WATERING Allow to dry between waterings

COMMENTS This old-fashioned plant is still a favorite for dish gardens and looks quite different from the newer compact *Philodendron* hybrids.

Janet Craig dracaena

Dracaena fragrans 'Janet Craig'

DESIGN USE Floor plant, desktop plant

SHAPES Wide columnar

HEIGHT/POT SIZE 12 inches tall in 6-inch pot, up to 5 to 6 feet in 14-inch pot

LIGHTING Low light

WATERING Allow to dry out between waterings

COMMENTS A workhorse of the interiorscape, used frequently in offices and atriums. Leaves are naturally glossy. Tends to develop fluoride toxicity in areas with high fluoride levels in the water. Grown in a bush form with three or more plants per pot. 'Limelight' looks similar but has neon green leaves, while 'Art' (synonym 'Carmen') has a yellow stripe along the leaf edge.

Janet Craig Compacta dracaena

Dracaena fragrans 'Janet Craig Compacta'

Synonym *Dracaena deremensis* 'Janet Craig Compacta'

DESIGN USE Desktop plant, floor plant if grown in cane form

SHAPES Columnar

HEIGHT/POT SIZE 12 inches tall in 6-inch pot, up to 6 to 8 feet tall in 14-inch pot when grown in cane form

LIGHTING Low light

WATERING Allow to dry out well between waterings

COMMENTS Has very compact ridged leaves on a thin narrow stem. 'Green Jewel' is a popular cultivar that looks like 'Janet Craig Compacta' but grows much larger.

Kentia palm

Howea forsteriana

DESIGN USE Floor plant, atriums, gardens

SHAPES Fan shaped

HEIGHT/POT SIZE 4 to 5 feet tall in 10-inch pot, up to 10 feet in 17-inch pot

LIGHTING Low light

WATERING Allow to dry somewhat between waterings

COMMENTS An expensive, slow-growing palm usually used in upscale offices and restaurants. Typically there are just a few large fronds per plant, with a clump of three to five plants or more per pot.

Lipstick vine

Aeschynanthus pulcher

Design use Hanging baskets, groundcover in garden, green walls

Shapes Vining

Height/Pot size Very low plant of long vines 2 to 4 inches tall in 6- to 10-inch pot

Lighting Bright indirect light

Watering Allow to dry somewhat between waterings

Comments Produces red tube-shaped flowers along the vines. Has thick waxy leaves. Goldfish vine (*Columnea* species) is similar but has yellow blooms.

Majesty palm

Ravenea rivularis

Design use Floor plant, atriums, gardens

Shapes Fan shaped, multiple fronds arising from the soil

Height/Pot size 6 feet tall in 12-inch pot, up to 12 to 15 feet in 17-inch pot

Lighting Bright indirect light to bright light

Watering Keep moist at all times, especially in higher light levels

Comments This palm will grow quickly in sun and may require subirrigation in higher light levels. Relatively inexpensive for its size and used often in atriums and lobbies.

Marginata, Madagascar dragon tree

Dracaena cincta

Synonym *Dracaena marginata*

Design use Desktop plant, floor plant, gardens, atriums, dish gardens, color bowls

Shapes Fan shaped or columnar depending on its size. Stems can be trained to grow in a candelabra form or other bent forms. Sometimes several stems are woven or braided together into a topiary form.

Height/Pot size 8 to 12 inches tall in 6-inch pot, up to 12- to 14-foot specimens. Cuttings are sometimes used in dish gardens.

Lighting Medium light

Watering Allow to dry out between waterings

Comments This plant can be pruned into interesting shapes and used as a focal point in gardens. Popular cultivars include 'Colorama' (red and pink leaves), 'Magenta' (burgundy leaves), 'Tarzan' (thick green leaves), and 'Tricolor' (pink, green, and white leaves). The colored forms need more light than the species and do not last as long indoors.

Mass cane, Corn plant

Dracaena fragrans 'Massangeana'

Design use Floor plant

Shapes Columnar cane form with multiple canes per pot

Height/Pot size 3 to 4 feet tall in 10-inch pot, up to 6 to 8 feet in 17-inch pot

Lighting Low light

Watering Allow to dry out well between waterings

Comments Has a yellowish stripe down the center of the leaf. May lose its variegation in lower light levels. Blooms if exposed to chilling temperatures, which ruins the symmetry of the plant. *Dracaena fragrans* has solid green leaves. 'Costaricana' has deeply ridged leaves, and 'Lisa' has long narrower leaves that tend to flop down. Other similar varieties and species are also available. The plant in the photo is a 10-inch, 4-3-2 mass cane; the heights of each cane from the floor to the top of the wood stem are 4 feet, 3 feet, and 2 feet tall, respectively.

Ming aralia
Polyscias fruticosa

DESIGN USE Most commonly as a floor plant, also used as a desktop plant or in miniature gardens

SHAPES Columnar

HEIGHT/POT SIZE 4 inches tall in 2- to 4-inch pot, 6 inches tall in 6-inch pot, up to 8 feet in 17-inch pot

LIGHTING Bright light

WATERING Keep evenly moist

COMMENTS Ming aralia has an oriental look and tends to be more expensive than plants of a similar size. Leaves may be fine and feathery, deeply crinkled or flat, depending on the species. Some are a deep burgundy in color. Aralia leaves tend to give off a distinct fragrance, especially on sunny days and when they are touched. Other popular varieties include *Polyscias balfouriana* (dinner plate aralia), and *P. scutellaria* 'Fabian'.

Natal mahogany
Trichilia dregeana

DESIGN USE Floor plant

SHAPES Columnar

HEIGHT/POT SIZE 4 to 5 feet tall in 10-inch pot, to 6 feet in 14-inch pot

LIGHTING Bright indirect light. Tolerates lower light levels once acclimated.

WATERING Keep moist

COMMENTS Foliage is a dark burgundy in high light. Plant can be temperamental about its watering. Susceptible to mealybugs and scale.

Neanthe bella palm, Parlor palm

Chamaedorea elegans

DESIGN USE Dish gardens, miniature gardens, fairy gardens, terrariums, desktop plant, floor plant, green walls

SHAPES Fan shaped

HEIGHT/POT SIZE 4 inches tall in 2-inch pot, up to 3 feet in 10-inch pot

LIGHTING Low light

WATERING Keep moist at all times

COMMENTS Seedlings are often used in miniature gardens and terrariums. Tends to get spider mites in hot sunny locations.

Nephthytis, 'White Butterfly' nephthytis

Syngonium podophyllum 'White Butterfly'

DESIGN USE Desktop plant, dish gardens, miniature gardens, green walls

SHAPES Clump shaped with a tendency to vining

HEIGHT/POT SIZE 6 inches tall in 2- to 4-inch pot, up to 12 inches in 10-inch pots with vines

LIGHTING Low to medium light

WATERING Allow to dry out a little between waterings

COMMENTS Variegated with white depending on the variety. May look weedy if allowed to vine. Primarily used in small sizes. The most common form of *Syngonium*.

Norfolk Island pine
Araucaria heterophylla

Design use Tree in gardens, atriums, holiday decor

Shapes Triangular

Height/Pot size 6 inches tall in 4-inch pot, to 6 to 8 feet in 14-inch pots, can also be used as a specimen

Lighting Bright light. Tolerates lower light levels.

Watering Keep moist at all times

Comments Used most often for the Christmas holidays due to its resemblance to a pine tree. Drops its branches if it dries out. Can grow 20 to 40 feet tall in sunny atriums indoors.

Peace lily, Spath
Spathiphyllum hybrids

Design use Desktop plant, floor plant, green walls

Shapes Fan shaped

Height/Pot size 8 to 10 inches tall in 6-inch pot, up to 3 to 4 feet in 17-inch pot

Lighting Low to medium light

Watering Do not allow to dry out between waterings

Comments Thick spoon-shaped leaves on a long petiole with no visible stem. Produces white single spoon-shaped spathes once the plant has absorbed enough light energy, blooming more often in higher levels of light. Notorious for drastically wilting if it dries out. Usually recuperates from wilting with some damage. Height varies with the variety; some plants remain small and compact. Some people are allergic to the pollen. The stamen should be removed to prolong blooming time. Popular hybrids include 'Mauna Loa' (the original form), 'Sensation' (with large leaves), 'Starlight' (miniature habit), and 'Taylor's Green' (slower growing; see photo).

Philodendron

Philodendron **'Imperial Red'**

DESIGN USE Desktop plant, masses or borders in atriums and gardens, green walls

SHAPES Clump shaped, remaining compact

HEIGHT/POT SIZE 6 to 12 inches tall in 6- to 10-inch pot

LIGHTING Medium light

WATERING Allow to dry somewhat between waterings

COMMENTS One of the most popular forms of philodendron. Hybrids are available in a variety of solid-colored leaves, from dark green to burgundy to purple. The plants remain compact, although they may become leggy in lower light levels or as the plant matures, and can be cut back. Potassium deficiencies may occur in higher light levels. Other popular hybrids include 'Brasil', 'Congo', 'Golden Xanadu', and 'Prince of Orange'.

Ponytail palm

Beaucarnea recurvata

Synonym *Nolina recurvata*

DESIGN USE Desktop plant, floor plant, dish gardens

SHAPES Cascading foliage on top of a bulbous stalk

HEIGHT/POT SIZE 6 inches tall in 4-inch pot, up to 4 foot specimen

LIGHTING High light. Tolerates lower light levels.

WATERING Allow to dry completely between waterings

COMMENTS Not a palm as the common name applies, but a succulent that stores water in its bulbous stem. Narrow foliage grows from the top, has sharp edges, and tends to curve or twist. Often grown as a novelty plant.

Pothos, Devil's ivy

Epipremnum aureum

Synonym *Scindapsus aureus*

Design use Desktop plant, tabletop plant, filler in color bowls, dish gardens, and fairy gardens, filler and groundcover in atriums and gardens, green walls

Shapes Vining, groundcover

Height/Pot size 8 inches tall before vining in 4- to 6-inch pot

Lighting Low light

Watering Allow to dry between waterings

Comments One of the most popular indoor plants, very easy to grow with few problems. Leaves are waxy and heart-shaped, and most varieties are variegated with white or yellow markings. If vines grow vertically upward, the leaves will grow larger as the vine grows taller. Most popular cultivars include 'Golden' (yellow markings), 'Jade' (solid green), 'Marble Queen' (white), and 'N'Joy' (smaller leaves with white markings).

Pygmy date palm

Phoenix roebelenii

Design use Floor plant, gardens

Shapes Fan shaped, may be on a solitary short trunk

Height/Pot size 3 to 4 feet tall in 10-inch pot, up to 4 to 5 feet in 17-inch pot, tends to stay fairly short

Lighting Bright indirect light

Watering Keep moist at all times. Do not allow to dry out.

Comments This palm has very sharp spines on its midribs with sharply pointed fronds with sharp edges and should be kept out of walkways. It tends to develop mites, scale, and mealybugs, which can be difficult to detect and control due to the narrow ridged fronds.

Reflexa, Ribbon plant

Dracaena reflexa

Synonym *Pleomele reflexa*

DESIGN USE Floor plant, atriums, gardens

SHAPES Wide columnar, stems may grow in interesting curved patterns

HEIGHT/POT SIZE 3 to 4 feet tall in 10-inch pot, up to specimens 10 to 12 feet tall

LIGHTING Medium light

WATERING Allow to dry out between waterings

COMMENTS Short strappy leaves on narrow stems. Cultivars include 'Song of India' (white stripes) and 'Song of Jamaica' (yellow stripes).

Rhapis palm, Lady palm, Lady finger palm

Rhapis excelsa

DESIGN USE Floor plant

SHAPES Columnar

HEIGHT/POT SIZE 4 to 5 feet tall in 10-inch pot, up to 6 to 8 feet in 17-inch pot

LIGHTING Low to medium light. Tolerates very low light levels for short periods.

WATERING Keep moist at all times unless in very low light (30 FC or less).

COMMENTS This palm is fairly expensive for its size and is usually used in upscale offices and residences. The petioles on the leaflets can become very long and stretched out in lower light levels. The genus name is sometimes spelled *Raphis* or *Rhapsis*.

Rikki dracaena

Dracaena deremensis **'Rikki'**

DESIGN USE Floor plant

SHAPES Fan shaped

HEIGHT/POT SIZE 12 inches tall in 6-inch pot, up to 2 feet in 10-inch pot

LIGHTING Low light

WATERING Allow to dry out between waterings

COMMENTS Very narrow strappy leaves. A hardy plant. Easy to maintain.

Rubber plant

Ficus elastica

DESIGN USE Desktop plant, floor plant, gardens

SHAPES Bush or tree form

HEIGHT/POT SIZE 2- to 3-feet tall bush in 10-inch pot, up to 8-foot tree in 17-inch pot

LIGHTING Medium light

WATERING Keep somewhat moist except in lower light levels

COMMENTS Many cultivars are available. The flat leaves may be green or burgundy in color. 'Burgundy' (see photo) is the most popular cultivar.

Sago palm, King sago palm

Cycas revoluta

DESIGN USE Focal point in gardens, floor plant

SHAPES Fan shaped

HEIGHT/POT SIZE 2 to 3 feet tall in 10-inch pot, up to 3 to 4 feet or more in 14- to 17-inch pot

LIGHTING Bright indirect light. Tolerates lower light levels for short periods.

WATERING Allow to dry somewhat between waterings

COMMENTS In sufficient light and if exposed to cooler temperatures, sago palm will develop a cone-shaped flower and will lose all of its needlelike leaves. It will grow a new set of leaves within a few weeks. Not a true palm, this plant dates back to prehistoric times.

Schefflera, Scheff, Umbrella plant

Schefflera actinophylla

Synonym *Brassaia actinophylla*

DESIGN USE Floor plant, gardens, atriums

SHAPES Wide columnar, tends to grow into a rectangular shape

HEIGHT/POT SIZE 3 to 4 feet tall in 10-inch pot, up to 6 to 7 feet in 14-inch pot. Specimens may also be available.

LIGHTING Medium light

WATERING Allow to dry somewhat between waterings

COMMENTS Clusters of large glossy leaves on a long petiole. 'Amate' (see photo) is the most common variety.

Snake plant, Mother-in-law tongue

Sansevieria species

DESIGN USE Desktop plant, dish gardens, short floor plant

SHAPES Spear shaped

HEIGHT/POT SIZE 4 inches tall in 4-inch pot, up to 2 to 3 feet in 14-inch pot

LIGHTING Low light

WATERING Allow to dry well between waterings

COMMENTS Does very well in very low light levels (30 FC). Leaves stand up from the soil and are very thick and waxy. A few varieties grow in rosettes close to the ground. All varieties have an underground stem system. Many different varieties are available with different colors and patterns of variegation. The most popular forms for interiorscapes are 'Black Gold' (deep black green), 'Laurentii' (yellow and green; see photo), *Sansevieria cylindrica* (cone-shaped leaves with green variegation), and *S. zeylanica* (yellow, green, and white).

Spider plant

Chlorophytum comosum

DESIGN USE Hanging baskets, tabletop plant, patioscapes, green walls

SHAPES Cascading

HEIGHT/POT SIZE 8- or 10-inch hanging basket or 4-inch tabletop plant

LIGHTING Medium light

WATERING Allow to dry between waterings

COMMENTS This is an old favorite houseplant with white stripes and cascades of "babies." Although hanging baskets have lapsed in popularity, you may find small spider plants on tabletops. They are a favorite choice for green walls.

Warneckii, Striped dracaena

Dracaena deremensis **'Warneckii'**

DESIGN USE Desktop plant, floor plant

SHAPES Fan shaped, or columnar if grown in cane form

HEIGHT/POT SIZE 6 to 12 inches tall in 6-inch pot, up to 6 to 8 feet if grown as a cane

LIGHTING Low to medium light

WATERING Allow to dry out between waterings

COMMENTS Many different varieties of striped dracaenas look similar to 'Warneckii', which has white stripes. Some of the more popular forms include 'Gold Star', 'Jade Jewel', 'Jumbo', 'Lemon Lime', 'Lemon Surprise' (leaves have a cork-screw twist with yellow variegation), and 'Whitney'. May also be spelled 'Warneckei', although most professional horticulturists now use the spelling 'Warneckii'.

Washington palm

Washingtonia robusta

DESIGN USE Focal points in gardens, tall atriums

SHAPES Round or fan shaped when young, growing into a solitary-trunked palm

HEIGHT/POT SIZE Anywhere from 4 feet when young in 10- to 14-inch pots, up to 20 feet or more tall as specimen trees

LIGHTING High light

WATERING Allow to dry somewhat between waterings

COMMENTS This species is mostly used as a tall specimen, solitary-trunked palm in an atrium and can easily grow 20 feet tall or more indoors. It can live for many years if cared for properly, often growing into the ceiling. It cannot be cut back without killing the tree, so eventually plants need to be replaced. Other types of fan palms include Chinese fan palm (*Livistona chinensis*) and European fan palm (*Chamaerops humilis*).

Weeping fig

Ficus benjamina

DESIGN USE Floor plant, atriums, gardens, desktop plant, dish gardens

SHAPES Bush or tree form

HEIGHT/POT SIZE 6-inch tall cuttings in 4-inch pots, up to specimen trees

LIGHTING Bright indirect light

WATERING Keep moist

COMMENTS Can be grown as a bush or tree form. Stems are sometimes braided or woven together to form a topiary tree. Invasive root system if used in a garden. Indian laurel fig (*Ficus nitida*) is similar but has thicker leaves and grows more compactly.

Yucca plant

Yucca gigantea
Synonym *Yucca elephantipes*

DESIGN USE Floor plant, gardens

SHAPES Fan shaped if grown one plant per pot. May be grown as a cane form with multiple canes in the same pot.

HEIGHT/POT SIZE 2 to 3 feet tall in 10-inch pot, up to 8 feet in 17-inch pot when grown in cane form

LIGHTING Bright light

WATERING Allow to dry well between waterings

COMMENTS A succulent with very sharply edged and sharply pointed leaves. Keep it out of walkways. It tends to develop eriophyid mites and coniothyrium, a black spotted fungal disease.

ZZ plant

Zamioculcas zamiifolia

DESIGN USE Desktop plant, floor plant, gardens, green walls

SHAPES Fan shaped

HEIGHT/POT SIZE 6 to 12 inches tall in 6-inch pot, up to 2 to 3 feet in 14-inch pot

LIGHTING Low to medium light

WATERING Allow to dry well between waterings

COMMENTS A very hardy plant. Tends to get leggy in lower light levels.

FLOWERING PLANTS

Note that most flowering plants are grown indoors for short periods. If plants are to be kept inside for less than one month, they can usually tolerate lower light levels.

Anthurium
Anthurium varieties

DESIGN USE Flowering plant, desktop plant, indoor gardens, tabletop plant, special occasion rentals, green walls

SHAPES Fan shaped

HEIGHT/POT SIZE 8 to 10 inches tall in 4-inch pot, to 18 inches in 6- to 7-inch pot

LIGHTING Medium light

WATERING Keep evenly moist

COMMENTS Anthuriums have a waxy "flower" (technically a shield-shaped modified leaf known as a spathe with a protruding spadix) in white, red, or pink and are frequently used during the Christmas and Valentine's Day holidays. 'Lady Jane' is pictured here.

Azalea

Rhododendron **hybrids**

DESIGN USE Color bowls, holiday displays

SHAPES Round or fan shaped

HEIGHT/POT SIZE 6 to 12 inches tall in 4- to 6-inch pot, sometimes available in 10-inch pot for outdoor use

LIGHTING Bright light

WATERING Keep evenly moist. Do not allow to dry out between waterings

COMMENTS Flowers will last for 10 days to two weeks. Keep cool to prolong flowering. Flowers may be solid-colored or variegated. Colors include white, pink, and red.

Bromeliad

Guzmania **hybrids**

DESIGN USE Color rotations, color bowls, special occasion rentals, desktop plant, gardens, green walls

SHAPES Fan shaped with a columnar flower spike

HEIGHT/POT SIZE 12- to 20-inch tall flower spike in 6-inch pot

LIGHTING Low to medium light

WATERING Water the soil (not the cup) and keep evenly moist

COMMENTS Flowers will last 10 to 12 weeks or more, the most commonly used flowering plant in commercial interiorscapes due to their longevity and variety of colors available. Guzmanias are the most widely used bromeliads in the interiorscape. Some popular hybrids are 'Flaming Sword', 'Kapoho Fire', 'Luna', 'Marjan' (see photo), and 'Ostara'. Other bromeliad genera include *Aechmea*, *Neoregelia*, *Tillandsia*, and *Vriesea*.

Caladium

Caladium **species and hybrids**

DESIGN USE As longer-term color in color bowls and gardens

SHAPES Columnar to fan shaped, leaves tend to droop as the plant grows older

HEIGHT/POT SIZE 12 to 18 inches tall in 6-inch pot

LIGHTING Bright indirect light

WATERING Keep evenly moist

COMMENTS Used for their colorful leaves as an alternative to flowering plants. Plants stay looking good from two to four weeks, up to several months, depending greatly on the amount of light and proper watering. Leaves are usually variegated and may include white, pink, green, and red, either in bands, splotches, or spotted. 'Sweetheart' (see photo) is a compact plant with slightly ruffled leaves.

Cyclamen

Cyclamen **species and hybrids**

DESIGN USE Color bowls, gardens

SHAPES Fan shaped

HEIGHT/POT SIZE 4 to 6 inches tall in 6-inch pot

LIGHTING Medium light

WATERING Keep evenly moist

COMMENTS Grown for its delicate-looking flowers. Prefers cooler temperatures. Flowers will last about two weeks, longer if kept cool. Flower colors include white, pink, magenta, and red.

Kalanchoe

Kalanchoe hybrids

DESIGN USE Color rotations, color bowls, special occasion rentals, desktop plant, gardens, green walls

SHAPES Round or slightly fan shaped

HEIGHT/POT SIZE 6 inches tall in 4-inch pot, up to 12 inches in 6-inch pot

LIGHTING Medium light

WATERING Allow to dry somewhat between waterings

COMMENTS Produces compact clusters of small flowers. A succulent. Flowers last four weeks or more. Available in a variety of colors including white, yellow, orange, pink, and red. Other varieties are grown for their interesting leaves.

Mum plant

Chrysanthemum varieties

DESIGN USE Color rotations, color bowls, special occasion rentals, desktop plant, gardens, patioscapes

SHAPES Round or slightly fan shaped

HEIGHT/POT SIZE 12 to 18 inches tall in 6-inch pot

LIGHTING Medium light

WATERING Keep evenly moist

COMMENTS A workhorse and old favorite. Flowers last two to four weeks depending on conditions. Mostly available as cushion mums or daisy mums in a variety of colors, including white, yellow, bronze, lavender, and deep purple. Excellent choice when a mass of color is needed.

Orchid, Moth orchid

Phalaenopsis hybrids

DESIGN USE Color bowls, special occasion rentals, desktop plant, gardens, green walls

SHAPES Cascading flower spike on rosette plant

HEIGHT/POT SIZE 18- to 24-inch long flower spike in 4- to 7-inch pot

LIGHTING Medium light

WATERING Keep evenly moist

COMMENTS Flowers will last four weeks or more depending on the conditions. Available in a variety of colors, mostly white with purple markings. Thousands of orchid hybrids and varieties are available today, those in the genus *Phalaenopsis* are the most popular for interiorscape use. Colors include white, yellow, lavender, pink, pale green, and purple. Flowers may be solid, variegated, or spotted.

Poinsettia

Euphorbia pulcherrima

DESIGN USE Color bowls, holiday displays

SHAPES Round or fan-shaped bush, or standard tree form

HEIGHT/POT SIZE Bush forms 6 inches tall in 4-inch pots, up to 30 inches in 10-inch pot. Standard tree forms usually 3 to 4 feet tall in 10- to 14-inch pots.

LIGHTING Medium light

WATERING Keep evenly moist. May allow the soil surface to dry out.

COMMENTS Needs protection from cold, drafts, and hot air vents. Has very delicate roots, leaves, and bracts. Do not drop or jostle around, as roots and stems break easily, leaves and bracts are easily damaged and bruised. Remove from boxes as soon as possible to prevent epinasty (permanent drooping). Bract colors include white, pale yellow, pale green, red, burgundy, and pink. Flowers may be solid colored, variegated, or spotted.

TRADE ASSOCIATIONS AND NON-PROFIT ORGANIZATIONS

The following organizations are involved in the interior plantscape industry and can provide additional information, resources, and a directory of their members and/or supporters.

Australia and New Zealand

INTERIOR PLANTSCAPE ASSOCIATION

interiorplantscape.asn.au

Canada

LANDSCAPE ONTARIO

landscapeontario.com

Europe

EUROPEAN INTERIOR LANDSCAPING ORGANISATION

eilo.eu

Japan

NIPPON (JAPAN) INDOOR GREEN ASSOCIATION

Can be contacted via Interior Plantscape Association in Australia

United Kingdom

EUROPEAN FEDERATION OF INTERIOR
LANDSCAPING GROUPS (EFIG)

efig.co.uk

United States

AMERICANHORT

americanhort.org

FLORIDA NURSERY, GROWERS AND
LANDSCAPE ASSOCIATION (FNGLA)

fngla.org

GREEN PLANTS FOR GREEN BUILDINGS
(GPGB)

gpgb.org

INTERIORSCAPE INDUSTRY COALITION

A collaboration between interior plantscape associations,
schools, and non-profit organizations in the United States
and Canada. Can be contacted through Green Plants for
Green Buildings or Landscape Ontario.

NATIONAL FOLIAGE FOUNDATION

nationalfoliagefoundation.org.

NATIONAL ASSOCIATION OF LANDSCAPE
PROFESSIONALS (formerly PLANET)

landscapeprofessionals.org

CERTIFICATION AND ACCREDITATION PROGRAMS

Green Earth—Green Plants

Certification program for businesses, projects and supplies for eco-friendly practices. Developed and administered by Johnson Fediw Associates as an independent third-party certification provider. More information can be found at greenearthgreenplants.com.

Landscape Industry Certified Technician-Interior

Landscape Industry Certified Manager-Interior

Certification for individuals. Under the management of the National Association of Landscape Professionals (formerly PLANET) in partnership with the Canadian Nursery Landscape Association. Other landscape-related certifications also available. More information can be found at landcarenetwork.org.

Accredited Member of IPA

Accreditation of IPA member companies, designating those businesses meeting strict regulations on safety, business practices, and other criteria. Developed and administered by the Interior Plantscape Association in Australia and New Zealand. More information can be found at ipa.asn.au.

Registered Trainer

Individuals are trained to provide specified programs to architects and other professionals for their credential renewals. Considered an educational program rather than a certification program. Developed and administered by Green Plants for Green Buildings. More information can be found at gpgb.org.

TRADE JOURNALS FOR INTERIOR PLANTSCAPING

Most of the trade associations and non-profit organizations send out email newsletters to their members and to the interested public. You may subscribe to these via their websites. Two other publications are worth noting here.

I-Plants Magazine

Monthly online magazine with articles, upcoming events, and new products for green walls and interior plantscape businesses. Distributed by email. Published by Johnson Fediw Associates. To subscribe and for past issues go to iplantsmagazine.com or interiorscapeconsultant.com.

Urban Horticulture Magazine

Monthly online magazine with articles, upcoming events, and new products for interior plantscaping, green walls, green roofs, and urban landscaping. For architects, interior designers, landscape businesses, landscape architects, interior plantscape businesses, and interested individuals. Distributed by email. Published by Johnson Fediw Associates. To subscribe and for past issues go to urbanhorticulture.com or interiorscapeconsultant.com

OTHER PUBLICATIONS BY THE AUTHOR

All of the resources listed here are available through the author's website at interiorscapeconsultant.com.

Online Courses

Online courses are available for individual or business use. Topics include Customer Service, Pricing Strategies, Palms, Dracaenas, Fungus Gnats, and How to be a Successful Technician. Please visit interiorscapeconsultant.com for the latest listings.

Green Plant Care Tips for Techs

Paperback book with guidelines on caring for indoor plants, beginner to intermediate level. Quizzes for each chapter, line drawings, and some color photos. A perfect companion book to this publication.

Plantscape 101

A six-class training manual on plant care, beginner level. Includes handouts, tests, answer sheets, diplomas, and so forth. Sold as a three-ring binder and/or CD. Includes the rights to make copies and use for an unlimited time.

Plantscape University

A ten-class training manual on plant care, intermediate level. Includes handouts, tests, answer sheets, diplomas, and so forth. Sold as a three-ring binder and/or CD. Includes the rights to make copies and use for an unlimited time.

Plantscape Masters

A ten-class training manual on plant care, advanced level. Includes handouts, tests, answer sheets, diplomas, and so forth. Sold as a three-ring binder and/or CD. Includes the rights to make copies and use for an unlimited time.

Hire and Train to Win

A human resource manual with many forms and templates for interior plantscape businesses. Includes detailed job descriptions, interview questions, personnel evaluation forms, disciplinary procedures, and so on. Includes the rights to make copies and use for an unlimited time.

Safety First

A safety guide for interior plantscape businesses and employees. Includes 21 safety topics with handouts, quizzes, and quiz answer sheets. For employee meetings and as a training manual. Includes the rights to make copies and use for an unlimited time.

CONVERSION TABLES

Inches (in.) to Centimeters (cm)

1/8 in.	0.1 cm
1/4 in.	0.6 cm
1 in.	2.5 cm
2 in.	5 cm
3 in.	8 cm
4 in.	10 cm
5 in.	13 cm
6 in.	15 cm
7 in.	18 cm
8 in.	20 cm
9 in.	23 cm
10 in.	25 cm
12 in.	30 cm
14 in.	36 cm
15 in.	38 cm
16 in.	40 cm
18 in.	45 cm
19 in.	48 cm
24 in.	60 cm
30 in.	76 cm
36 in.	91 cm

Feet (ft.) to Meters (m)

1/2 ft.	0.15 m
1 ft.	0.3 m
2 ft.	0.6 m
3 ft.	0.9 m
4 ft.	1.2 m
5 ft.	1.5 m
6 ft.	1.8 m
7 ft.	2.1 m
8 ft.	2.4 m
9 ft.	2.7 m
10 ft.	3 m
12 ft.	3.6 m
14 ft.	4.2 m
15 ft.	4.5 m
20 ft.	6 m
25 ft.	7.6 m
30 ft.	9 m
40 ft.	12 m
60 ft.	18 m
100 ft.	30 m

Square Feet to Square Meters

100 square ft.	9 square m

Temperature (°Fahrenheit to °Celsius)

32°F	0°C
40°F	4°C
45°F	7°C
50°F	10°C
55°F	13°C
60°F	15°C
65°F	18°C
75°F	24°C
78°F	26°C
115°F	46°C
120°F	49°C

BIBLIOGRAPHY AND RECOMMENDED READING

Associated Landscape Contractors of America. 2003. *The Guide to Interior Landscape Specifications*. 5th ed. Herdon Virginia: ALCA (now NALP).

Bergs, John. 2002. "Effect of Healthy Workplaces on Well-being and Productivity of Office Workers." In *Proceedings of International Plants for People Symposium*. Floriade, Amsterdam, Netherlands.

Brinsglimark, Tina, Terry Hartig, and Grete Grindal Patil. 2007. "Psychological Benefits of Indoor Plants in Workplaces: Putting Experimental Results into Context." *HortScience* 42(3): 581–587. http://hortsci .ashspublications.org/content/42/3/581.full.pdf

Costa, P. R, and R. W. James. 1995a. "Environmental Engineering Benefits of Plants." In *Proceedings of the Workplace Comfort Forum*. London, United Kingdom.

Costa, P., and R. W. James. 1995b. "Constructive Use of Vegetation in Office Buildings." Paper presented at the Plants for People Symposium, The Hague, Netherlands.

Costa, P., and R. W. James. 1999. "Air Conditioning and Noise Control Using Vegetation." In *Proceedings of the 8th International Conference on Indoor Air Quality and Climate*. Edinburgh, Scotland. 3: 234–239.

Costa, Peter. N.d. *Silence of the Palms*. Tropical Plants Information Leaflet 166. Rentokil Initial, Research & Development Department.

DiLaura, David, Kevin Houser, Richard Mistrick, and Gary Steffy, eds. 2011. *The Lighting Handbook*. 10th ed. New York: Illuminating Engineering Society.

Energy Independence and Security Act of 2007. 42 U.S.C. §17001.

Evans, Gary W. 2003. "The Built Environment and Mental Health." *Journal of Urban Health* 80(4): 536–555. http://www.ncbi.nlm.nih.gov/pmc/articles /PMC3456225/

Evert, Ray F., and Susan E. Eichhorn. 2013. *Raven Biology of Plants*. 8th ed. New York: W. H. Freeman and Company. p. 687.

Fjeld, Tøve. 1998. "Do Plants in Offices Promote Health?" Agricultural University of Norway. http://www. urbangarden.co.nz/pdfs/potted-plant-microcosm -office-field-study.pdf

Fjeld, Tøve. 2002. "The Effects of Plants and Artificial Daylight on the Well-being and Health of Office Workers, School Children, and Health-care Personnel." In *Proceedings of the International Plants for People Symposium*. Floriade, Amsterdam, Netherlands.

Fjeld, Tøve., B. Veiersted, L. Sandvik, G. Riise, and F. Levy. 1998. "The Effect of Indoor Foliage Plants on Health and Discomfort Symptoms Among Office Workers." *Indoor and Built Environment* 7(4):

204–209. http://horttech.ashspublications.org/content/10/1/46.full.pdf

Florida Foliage Association. 1982. *Guidelines to Foliage Plant Specifications for Interior Use*. Orlando, Florida: Florida Foliage Association (now Florida Nursery, Growers and Landscape Association).

Gaines, Richard L. 1977. *Interior Plantscaping: Building Design for Interior Foliage Plants*. New York: Architectural Record Books.

Greulach, Victor A., and J. Edison Adams. 1976. *Plants: An Introduction to Modern Botany*. 3rd ed. New York: John Wiley & Sons.

Griffith Jr., Lynn P. 2002. *Tropical Foliage Disorders: A Ball Guide to Diagnosis and Treatment*. Batavia, Illinois: Ball Publishing.

Heerwagen, Judith H. 2003. "Bio-Inspired Design: What Can We Learn from Nature?" *BioInspire* 1. Seattle, Washington: J. H. Heerwagen & Associates. 9 pp.

Kaplan, R., and S. Kaplan. 1990. "Restorative Experience: The Healing Power of Nearby Nature." In *The Meaning of Gardens: Idea, Place and Action*. Edited by M. Francis and R. T. Hester Jr. Cambridge, Massachusetts: MIT Press. 238–243.

Kaplan, S. 1995. "The Restorative Benefits of Nature: Towards an Integrative Framework." *Journal of Environmental Psychology* 15: 169–182.

Lohr, V. I., and C. H. Pearson-Mims. 2000. "Physical Discomfort May Be Reduced in the Presence of Interior Plants." *HortTechnology* 10(1): 53–58. http://public.wsu.edu/~lohr/hih/pain/

Lohr, V. I., C. H. Pearson-Mims, and G. K. Goodwin. 1996. "Interior Plants May Improve Worker Productivity and Reduce Stress in a Windowless Environment." *Journal of Environmental Horticulture* 14(2): 97–100. http://public.wsu.edu/~lohr/hih/productivity/

Park, S. H., R. H. Mattson, and E. Kim E. 2002. "Pain Tolerance Effects of Ornamental Plants in a Simulated Hospital Patient Room." *Acta Horticulturae* 639: 50–52.

Russell, George K., ed. 1991. "Arousing Biophilia: A Conversation with E. O. Wilson." *Orion Magazine* (winter). Orion Society.

Sandifer, Steven, and Baruch Givoni. 2002. "Thermal Effects of Vines on Wall Temperatures—Comparing Laboratory and Field Collected Data." SOLAR 2002, *Proceedings of the Annual Conference of the American Solar Energy Society*. Reno, Nevada. http://www.sbse.org/awards/docs/Sandifer.pdf

Shibata, S., and N. Suzuki. 2002. "Effects of Foliage Plants on Task Performance and Mood." *Journal of Environmental Psychology* 22 (3): 265–272. http://www.ingentaconnect.com/content/ap/ps/2002/00000022/00000003/art00232

Tarran, Jane, Fraser Torpy, and Margaret Burchett. 2007. "Use of Living Pot-Plants to Cleanse Indoor Air—Research Review." In *Proceedings of the 6th International Conference on Indoor Air Quality, Ventilation, and Energy Conservation in Building—Sustainable Built Environment*. Sendai, Japan. 3: 249–256.

Ulrich, Roger S. 1979. "Visual Landscapes and Psychological Well-being." *Landscape Research* 4(1): 17–23.

University of Minnesota, Twin Cities Campus, College of Design, Center for Sustainable Building Research. 2011. "Window Technologies: Glass." In *Windows for High-Performance Commercial Buildings*. Last modified on 18 October 2013. Retrieved from www.commercialwindows.org/vt.php.

Wolf, Kathleen L. 2002. "Retail and Urban Nature: Creating a Consumer Habitat." A paper submitted for the 2002 Plants for People Symposium, Amsterdam, Netherlands. http://www.plants-for-people.org/eng/science/

ACKNOWLEDGMENTS

There are many people to thank, who contributed to the completion and success of this book. First, I want to acknowledge the role that my Heavenly Father played in this project, who created plants not only for our enjoyment, but to sustain life on this planet. With Him all things are possible, including this book.

My dear husband, Ted Fediw, provided encouragement and support throughout the entire process, often stepping in to help with "life stuff" as each deadline approached. His support made it possible for me to write this book. My parents, Julia Johnson and my late father, Donald Johnson, also gave me their love and support throughout this project.

My editor, Tom Fischer, first contacted me about writing this book and then led me through the entire editing and publication process, putting his finishing touches on the manuscript. Thank you for the opportunity, Tom. Thanks also to Linda Willms for editorial support.

And a big thank you to my many clients, colleagues, and magazine subscribers, who contributed photographs of their projects and supplies to this book. A special thanks to Joseph Cialone at Tropical Computers, who contributed most of the photographs in the plant palette section of this book.

Friends, this one is for you.

Contributing Companies and Individuals

Architectural Supplements/ASIEarthforms
Atria
Beneficial Insectary
Botanicus Interior Landscaping
Calvert's Plant Interiors
Cityscapes
Clayton Hauck
Evergreen Interiors
Exaco Trading Company/Elho
Foliage Design Systems, Central Florida office
Green Connection
Greenjeans Interiorscape
Greentech Innovations
Harding Botanicals
Heroman Services Plant Company
Ian Drummond
Interior Plantscapes (Washington DC area)
Jay Scotts Company
John Mini Distinctive Landscapes
Kelly Mac Interiorscapes
LiveWall
Longwood Gardens
Lotus Gardenscapes

McCaren Designs
Mimosa Interior Landscape
Moore Landscapes
Morning Dew Tropical Plants
No Sweat! Waterproof Liners
Parker Plants
Paul van der Wal, AIA
Peter Shields at PJS Plantscape Design
Phillips Interior Plants & Displays
Plant Solutions
Planterra (Canada)
Scott Creamer
SFO Landscaping
SNIPS Landscape & Nursery
Sunshine Tropical Foliage
Sylvia Doner and Plantarium Living
    Environments
Tournesol Siteworks
Tropical Computers
The Urban Botanist
Waterboy/Plant-Tech H2O
Woolly Pocket Garden Company

PHOTOGRAPHY AND DESIGN CREDITS

Photographs and designs are by the author except for the following:

McRae Anderson, ALSA, photographer and designer for McCaren Designs, pages 39, 40 top and bottom, 68, 102, 124 bottom, 138, 146, 151, 157.

Keith Behringer, John Mini Distinctive Landscapes, page 158.

Jean Berg, **Clayton Hauck**, and **Shannon McCormick**, photographers for Phillips Interior Plants & Displays, pages 14, 15, 28, 65 right, 70, 71, 101, 104, 107, 122 top, 123, 126 right, 175.

Sonya Broughton, Department of Agriculture & Food Western Australia, Bugwood.org, page 190 bottom.

Michael Cabrera, photographer for Moore Landscapes, pages 13 top, 26, 73, 124 top, 177.

Jeeheon Cho, photographer, and **Sarah Stalker** and **Katherine Gordon**, designers, for Lotus Gardenscapes, pages 67 top left, 128.

Joseph Cialone, photographer for Tropical Computers, pages 200–202, 203 left, 204–226, 227 right, 228–229.

R. Andrew Cook for Exaco Trading Company/Elho green wall products, page 142.

B. Scott Creamer for Evergreen Interiors, page 119.

Marcée Cretarolo, photographer for SFO Landscaping, page 72.

Bruce A. Crowle, photographer for Atria, pages 62, 161.

Steve Decker, photographer for Architectural Supplements/ASI Earthforms, pages 82 bottom, 84 bottom, 85 bottom, 86 left and right, 88 bottom left, 89 bottom left, right top and bottom, 90 left and right, 91

Sylvia Doner, photographer and designer, for Plantarium Living Environments, page 155.

Ian Drummond, page 112.

Eric Emerton, photographer for Green Connection, pages 121 bottom, 130, 131, 133.

Patricia Evans, Communications Director for Longwood Gardens, page 147.

Janice Goodman, photographer for Cityscapes, pages 118, 129.

Greenjeans Interiorscape, Michael Martens photographer, page 80.

Mary Ann Hansen, Virginia Polytechnic Institute and State University, Bugwood.org, page 185.

Beth Harding, photographer for Harding Botanicals, page 13 bottom.

Deborah Heroman, photographer for Heroman Services Plant Company, page 16.

Peter Herrera, photographer for No Sweat! Waterproof Liners, page 111 left.

Chazz Hesselein, Alabama Cooperative Extension System, Bugwood.org, page 188.

hvoya, shutterstock, page 227 left.

Kevin Kelly, photographer and designer for Kelly Mac Interiorscapes, pages 140, 156.

Mike Lewis for Foliage Design Systems, Central Florida office, pages 18, 96, 109.

Denis Lincoln, photographer, and Wendy Bosbach, designer, for Everything Grows Interior Landscape, pages 65 left, 116, 120, 122 bottom right.

MACGroup, Sara Roberts, Concierge Services, page 46.

Dave MacKenzie, photographer for LiveWall, page 153.

C. Moorlander, photographer for Beneficial Insectary, pages 189, 191 top and bottom.

Ettore Mormile, photographer for Interior Plantscapes (Washington DC area), pages 21 top and bottom, 25, 31, 67 bottom, 100, 126 left.

John E. Moses, photographer for Architectural Supplements/ASI Earthforms, pages 81, 85 left, 87, 89 top left.

Pekka Nikonen, shutterstock, page 203 right.

Kathryn O'Donnell, photographer for Botanicus Interior Landscaping, pages 32 right, 108, 110.

Keith Rinearson, photographer for Calvert's Plant Interiors, pages 32 left, 69.

Angel Rebolledo for Jay Scotts Company, pages 82 top, 84 top, 88 top left and bottom right.

Stephen Rowson, photographer for The Urban Botanist, page 134.

Pete Shields, photographer and designer for PJS Plantscape Design, page 154.

Sunshine Tropical Foliage, James Jacob, page 122 bottom left.

Osram Sylvania, Michael Foote, Senior Creative Specialist and Visuals Coordinator, page 49.

Leslie C. Thompson for Planterra (Canada), page 41.

Paul van der Wal, AIA, architect designer and photoapher, pages 36, 37.

Stephen VanHorn, shutterstock, page 44.

Paul Zaccarine, photographer for Mimosa Interior Landscape, page 20.

Joe Zazzera, photographer for Plant Solutions, pages 149, 152.

INDEX

ABOUT THE AUTHOR

Kathy Fediw is an internationally known interior plantscape consultant, author, and speaker with over 30 years' experience. She is a LEED Accredited Professional, a Certified Landscape Professional, and a Certified Landscape Technician. The company she started provides consulting services, training workshops, online courses, and other educational resources to interior plantscaping businesses worldwide.

Author of *Green Plant Care Tips for Techs* as well as a series of training manuals and online courses, Kathy also publishes and edits two monthly online magazines, *I-Plants* and *Urban Horticulture*, and is a frequent speaker on horticulture, management, and green building topics in the United States and elsewhere. She developed the Green Earth–Green Plants certification program for eco-friendly horticultural businesses, and is actively involved with various trade associations across the country.

Kathy is an accomplished artist and exhibits at several galleries in the greater Houston area where she lives. She has a Bachelor of Science degree from Penn State University. Visit her website at InteriorscapeConsultant.com.

J. MINER, QP STUDIOS